# EVALUATION OF A NURSING-LED IN-PATIENT SERVICE

# EVALUATION OF A NURSING-LED IN-PATIENT SERVICE

PETER GRIFFITHS • AMANDA EVANS

Published by the King's Fund Centre
126 Albert Street
London
NW1 7NF
Tel: 0171-267 6111



ISBN 1 85717 091 1

A CIP catalogue record for this book is available from the British Library

Distributed by Bournemouth English Book Centre (BEBC)
PO Box 1496
Poole
Dorset
BH12 3YD

The King's Fund Centre is a service development agency which promotes improvements in health and social care. We do this by working with people in health and social services, in voluntary agencies, and with the users of these services. We encourage people to try out new ideas, provide financial or practical support to new developments, and enable experiences to be shared through workshops, conferences, information services and publications. Our aim is to ensure that good developments in health and social care are widely taken up. The King's Fund Centre is part of the King's Fund.

# Contents

# Acknowledgements

The work presented here, including the development of the nursing-led service itself, would not have been possible without a great deal of commitment from managers and clinicians within King's Healthcare. It is they who have provided the majority of the support and funding for the project. It is also they who have taken the majority of the risks involved in allowing such an innovation to proceed.

The research conducted so far has mostly been undertaken without funding and has only been possible due to the presence of a researcher funded by King's Healthcare for the past three years. During the first two years the post was part-funded from a grant awarded to the unit by the King's Fund from the Sainsbury Family Trust in 1989 as one the four 'first wave' Nursing Development Units (NDUs) supported by their Nursing Developments Programme. Perhaps more important has been the hard work and forbearance of the ward's staff who have contributed considerable time and effort in order to provide data for the main study.

The unit has received invaluable support from both within and without King's Healthcare. The management and clinicians of the medical care group were not only prepared to take the risk of allowing the unit to go ahead, but also recognised the necessity of evaluating the initiative by supporting the research both by referring patients and by continuing to support the research post. The Executive Nursing and Quality Team has always been willing to provide assistance and support.

Externally, South East Thames Regional Health Authority provided a small grant to support a post for the first year of the project, which assisted in developing the referral and screening processes. Barbara Vaughan of the King's Fund has continued to provide considerable support, above and beyond the call of duty, as a member of the steering group for the NDU. Her help in preparing this manuscript is much appreciated. Many others have also committed a great deal of time and enthusiasm to the unit through this forum. Invaluable advice, insight and support throughout this new phase of the unit's development have been forthcoming; in particular, from Lynn Batehup who, as clinical leader, was involved in establishing the ward as an NDU and Professor Adrian Eddleston, a constant ally among our medical colleagues.

Professor Wilson-Barnett of the Department of Nursing Studies, King's College London, has provided academic support for the research as well as funding fees for postgraduate study. Peter Milligan of King's College London advised on statistical analyses and provided valuable insight into the appropriate interpretation of the data. The authors of the Nottingham Health Profile generously gave permission for us to use the new NHPD in the course of this study.

Finally, none of the work reported here would have been possible without the staff of Byron Ward. In particular, those who have acted as primary nurses for the 'nurse-managed' patients: Alyson Turner and Jonathan Williams. Ruth Harris acted as primary nurse for some of the first patients and was ward manager throughout the period covered by this report. Sadie Collison and Tracy Barlow worked with the referring teams to ensure the steady flow of patients to the unit, a frequently thankless task. The burden of collecting much of the research data has fallen on Sadie while Tracy, in addition to collecting data, conducted some of the interviews quoted in the final sections of this report. To them and the many other staff of the unit – our thanks and congratulations.

# EXECUTIVE SUMMARY

This report provides a companion to an earlier volume 'The Development of a Nursing-Led In-Patient Service' (Evans & Griffiths, 1994). The earlier volume provides an overview of the work undertaken in developing the service and the rationale for it. The focus of this volume is on giving more concrete information on the operation of the service using data collected during the course of the first 18 months of the project.

Central to the evaluation work carried out has been a pilot evaluation of patient outcomes by means of a randomised controlled trial. The hypothesis under investigation was that admission to the nursing-led ward will result in patient outcomes which are no different from current services, considering a range of variables including length of stay, overall health status, psychological well-being, physical dependence during hospital stay and after discharge, readmission rates, nursing-related complications and mortality.

This report describes the study, including information about the services offered, the sample group and the clinical outcomes. The methodological difficulties encountered are also described. Although the results to date are encouraging, further work is still needed to draw conclusive recommendations.

Outlined below is a summary of this report:

## *Chapter 1*

Previous work, in particular research conducted in the Oxfordshire NDUs, demonstrated the potential for nurses to manage in-patients and suggested that 'nurse-managed care' may have a positive impact on outcomes for those patients who remain in hospital but do not require acute medical services.

With increasing evidence that a proportion of acute medical beds are occupied by patients who do not require acute medical care (Audit Commission, 1992; Victor et al., 1994), this case is strengthened.

## *Chapter 2*

Byron NDU has offered a nursing-led service to a variety of in-patient groups since February 1993. The nursing-led service is based on a 13-bedded ward, shortly to increase to 23 beds.

The aim of the unit is to allow for the focus of nursing care to change from acutely ill patients to the therapeutic needs of non-acute patients.

This change of focus was anticipated to impact on a range of client outcomes including psychological well-being, physical dependence and the complications of immobility such as infection and pressure sores.

Patients are referred by a consultant physician, either directly or via a multi-disciplinary team meeting and assessed for suitability by a senior nurse from the NDU.

During the period covered by this report the majority of patients (n = 132) were referred from acute medical wards. It is hoped to expand the service in the near future.

Once a patient is accepted, transfer is arranged; there was a mean delay of 2.5 days after the patient was ready.

Care is managed by a primary nurse with support from the full multi-disciplinary team. Of patients, 91% (n = 70) received physiotherapy and 84% (n = 62) occupational therapy. The unit provides the same level of therapy input as provided on acute wards. The nursing establishment is calculated using the same formula used to determine staffing on acute medical wards.

There is no routine involvement from consultant physicians or their team. For the period covered in this report, routine medical care was provided by a general practitioner in four sessions per week, each of two hours.

## *Chapter 3*

Suitable patients are not defined by medical diagnosis. They must be medically stable but in need of further therapeutic input prior to discharge.

The core client groups referred to the service are those requiring rehabilitation following cerebrovascular accident (CVA; 29%, n = 28) or injury (23%, n = 16) which has led to a reduction in functional ability. In 15% of cases (n = 14) the reason for admission was a decline in functional status, in some cases independent of any medical diagnosis.

The emphasis on 'rehabilitation' as the reason for referral to the unit was not expected. Preliminary work identified 'education' as the most frequent need among the client group. It is unclear whether the use of the term rehabilitation is a reflection of client need or a blanket term applied to all non-medical needs by referrers.

Other frequent diagnostic categories admitted to the unit are patients with cardiac problems, and infections. Again, the reason for referral to Byron is usually given as rehabilitation.

It is interesting to note that, following assessment by the Byron staff, significantly more patient needs were identified in 25% (n = 24) of cases.

Key client groups identified as suitable for the service include those requiring education, wound management, and nurse-managed or initiated therapeutic programmes or assessment related to areas such as continence, constipation, pain, nutrition or discharge planning.

The service is not age-related but the client group is predominately elderly, with a mean age of 76 years.

Most have been admitted to hospital from their own home (86%, n = 102) or sheltered accommodation (7%, n = 8).

## *Chapter 4*

The phase one evaluation included a pilot study in which all patients were randomised into treatment or control groups prior to consideration for the unit. The control group remained under medically managed care, generally on acute medical wards. Some selective attrition occurred from the control group which reduced the control sample to 48 patients; there were 71 in the treatment group.

Results from this study indicate that patients managed on Byron are significantly more likely to be discharged back to their own home or sheltered accommodation than the control group. Despite this difference, the readmission rates are the same for the treatment and control group.

Transfer to Byron does not increase length of hospital stay. Corrected for differences in physical dependence, patients transferred to Byron stay in hospital for 47 days after referral to the unit; the control group 68 days. This difference is not statistically significant. There is a large variation in length of stay with the shortest length of stay being 2 days. Transfer to Byron appears to have most impact on the length of stay of patients who are less physically dependent.

Estimated saving in acute bed use is an average of 35–49 days per patient, assuming that Byron has no impact on overall length of stay.

There are no significant differences in mortality between patients cared for on Byron and those in the control group. The incidence of complications related to immobility – chest infection, urinary tract infection (UTI) and pressure sores – are significantly lower on Byron. These differences are reflected by increased physical independence at discharge from Byron when compared with the control group. This difference is not significant.

There are no differences between treatment and control groups in respect of input from paramedical professions.

Patients on Byron receive significantly less medical input. In particular there is a fourfold reduction in routine medical reviews.

Although all statistical tests were 'corrected' for pre-test scores, the results are encouraging but must be viewed with caution due to the attrition from the control group.

## *Chapter 5*

Although there have been difficulties in explaining the nature of the work on Byron to other professions, there has been a considerable degree of support and understanding.

There is still a considerable challenge in defining and communicating the nature of the service offered by Byron.

The Department of Health is funding an extended replication of the outcomes study, commencing in spring 1995.

# BACKGROUND

CHAPTER one

## Introduction

This report outlines the work of the nursing-led in-patient service on Byron Ward Nursing Development Unit (NDU), a part of King's Healthcare NHS Trust, during the first 18 months since its inception. At that time it was recognised that there was a critical need to evaluate the impact of the service in relation to patient outcomes. Central to the evaluation work was a pilot study, employing a randomised controlled trial to explore the hypothesis that:

**Admission to the nursing-led ward will result in patient outcomes which are no different from those achieved through current services.**

The variables used to assess this hypothesis included length of stay, overall health status, psychological and physiological well-being, physical dependence during hospital stay and at discharge, readmission rates, nursing-related complications and mortality.

The rationale for establishing the service and an outline of the steps which were taken in developing it are already available in a companion publication 'The Development of a Nursing-Led In-Patient Service' (Evans & Griffiths, 1994). This volume includes more concrete information on the manner in which the service was operationalised, alongside details of the evaluative work and the findings from the preliminary study.

## Background

The work of the NDU in developing a nursing-led service could be said to have been inspired by the work of the NDUs at Burford Community Hospital and, in particular, Beeson Ward at the Radcliffe Infirmary, Oxford. Both these units aimed to maximise the therapeutic potential of nursing for patients who were admitted to the units (Pearson, 1992; Pearson et al., 1992). This aim could be said to be the proper ultimate aim of any development of nursing practice or indeed any action carried out by nurses for the benefit of their patients. NDUs are defined as being 'committed to... maximising the therapeutic potential of nursing' (King's Fund Centre, 1989, quoted in Turner Shaw & Bosanquet, 1993 p.2). The defining feature of the Oxford units was the concept of 'nursing beds'.

'Therapeutic nursing' (McMahon, 1991; Pearson, 1989) can exist in any environment in which nursing takes place. The variety of clinical areas in which

NDUs have been established is testament to the belief of many nurses that the therapeutic dimension of nursing is common to many if not all aspects of nursing care. The King's Fund NDU programme now encompasses specialities as diverse as forensic psychiatry, intensive care, oncology, accident and emergency, and occupational health.

The Oxford work was aimed at maximising the therapeutic potential of nursing for a particular in-patient group. Pearson et al. (1992) argued that the therapeutic dimension of nursing was potentially lost in acute care settings. They argued that 'high level' technological medical and paramedical intervention predominated in acute settings, preventing nurses from focusing on the 'core' nursing roles of caring and nurturing which are in themselves therapeutic. Building in turn on the work of the Loeb Centre for Nursing and Rehabilitation in New York (Hall, 1969), they argued for units which focus upon the provision of nursing as therapy. 'Nursing beds' are defined as hospital space in which 'nursing is the chief therapy and the nurse is the chief therapist' (Tiffany, 1977, quoted in Pearson, 1989 p. 125).

There are three strands to the thesis proposed for the Oxfordshire units. First that there exists a therapeutic dimension for nursing. Second, that the need for therapeutic nursing predominates for certain patients in certain circumstances. Third, that the therapeutic dimension of nursing can only be fully realised by managing patient care and the nursing workload in a separate unit, with nurses given autonomy and full accountability for the provision of nursing care. This thesis led to the establishment of units where nurses were given full responsibility for patient care. Patients were transferred to this unit at a point where the 'biological crisis', necessitating acute medical services, had subsided in order to receive the benefit of fully therapeutic nursing care. The three propositions will be examined separately.

## The therapeutic dimensions of nursing

Pearson (Pearson, 1989; Pearson et al., 1992) cites work demonstrating the effect which nurses giving full information to patients has on post-operative recovery, e.g. Hayward (1975), and the benefits which accrue to patients through so-called 'therapeutic touch' (Tutton, 1991). Such interventions are not unique to nursing, however, and the therapeutic activity described could be usefully applied in a variety of caring settings by many professionals. Perhaps more instructive is Kitson's work (Kitson, 1986, 1991) which delineates the application of nursing care to the patient in a therapeutic manner using the framework of self-care activities described by Orem (1990). Kitson described how nursing activity can range from optimally therapeutic to minimally therapeutic. The prime focus of this work is patient's self-care activities or, to use an alternative terminology, activities of daily living.

*'The goal of care was seen to be the maintenance of the patient at the optimal level of self-care. Actions therefore that overlooked the patients capabilities or did not encourage him to use certain self-care skills were seen as non-therapeutic. Also, nursing activity that denied the patient the opportunity of making decisions…was seen as non-therapeutic, as were actions that made him more dependent…' (Kitson, 1991 p. 172).*

It is this 'quality' of nursing which is seen as the core of 'therapeutic nursing'. Thus, in assisting the patient to perform self-care activities, nursing can be a therapeutic force. Miller's (1985) study identified the consequences of non-individualised care for elderly patients. She identified physical dependence in patients as an iatrogenic condition caused by traditional modes of nursing care. This study illustrates the therapeutic potential in nursing by reference to its absence.

If physical dependence is typified as an iatrogenic condition, consequent upon 'non-therapeutic' nursing, one must quickly extend the therapeutic domains of nursing to that of psychological well-being. McSweeney (1991) described a large body of work which could be said to delineate the consequences of non-therapeutic nursing intervention in terms of patient distress. Barder et al. (1994) described the vulnerability of elderly people to depression through learned helplessness which is in turn mediated through the promotion of physical dependence. Given the high level of psychological distress which exists in hospitalised patients, the intervention of nursing could be a positive or negative force.

## The changing needs of hospital in-patients

Ersser (1988) described the range of non-medical health care needs which may require further hospitalisation (or other therapy) after the patient has become medically stable. To put it most simply, Ersser argued that health needs are not synonymous with medical needs. Many of the areas described are those in which nursing may have a therapeutic influence, such as regaining independence, attaining knowledge about new conditions or handicap, and adjustment to such disability.

Estimates of the proportion of patients in hospital who do not require acute medical care vary, but range from 15% of all in-patients to 48% of acute medical in-patients (Audit Commission, 1992; Victor et al., 1994). The needs of these patients vary enormously. Although some of these patients are waiting for discharge, either due to delays in decision making or the arrangement of appropriate community services or placement (Audit Commission, 1992; Semke et al., 1989; Victor et al., 1994), the majority are awaiting or receiving some other therapeutic input. For many, this therapy must be delivered in a hospital setting because of the patient's need for supportive or therapeutic nursing care.

## The therapeutic nursing unit

The hypothesis behind the creation of the 'clinical nursing unit' (Pearson, 1983) was that for many patients it is therapeutic nursing care which is the major determinant of their recovery. This hypothesis could be extended by adding that, for many patients, it is the presence or absence of therapeutic nursing which is a major determinant of recovery or lack of it. The distinction may appear to be obvious but the extension of the hypothesis emphasises the potential for nursing to combine with the work of other therapists in a positive or negative fashion, particularly (but not exclusively) in the area of physical rehabilitation.

Pearson argues that the therapeutic aspects of nursing are impeded by the contrasting demands made on nurses' time in acute areas. The rationale for grouping the patients into a single 'Clinical Nursing Unit' was 'to create a unit where an ideology of therapeutic nursing could prevail' (Pearson et al., 1992 p. 2).

## Testing the concept: evaluating the therapeutic nursing unit

Ersser (1988) reviewed two studies evaluating the 'effectiveness' of 'nursing beds'. One unpublished study (Hall et al., 1975) cited in Ersser (1988) found that patients randomly assigned to the 'nursing-led' unit had more favourable outcomes of hospital care than a control group cared for in a conventional hospital. Patients of New York's Loeb centre were less frequently hospitalised and more likely to return to work than the control group but had similar outcomes in terms of functional ability and mortality. Total length of hospital stay was increased but costs of hospitalisation were reduced.

In Pearson's pilot evaluation of nursing-led beds in a community hospital (subsequently described in Pearson et al., 1992), 45 patients were randomly assigned to the nursing beds in a community hospital. Outcomes were compared with a control group who remained in the acute care setting. The control group comprised 25 patients who agreed to transfer but were randomly allocated to a control group and 82 patients who refused transfer. The study group comprised elderly patients who had undergone internal fixation for fractured neck of femur. No difference was noted in total length of hospital stay. However, patients discharged from the nursing unit had lower levels of physical dependence than controls although this difference was not statistically significant. 'Life satisfaction' was significantly higher in the treatment group as was satisfaction with care. The author warned of a need for caution owing to the small sample size and a 'simple' randomisation technique (Pearson et al., 1992 p. 12).

The extended replication of the pilot study (Pearson et al., 1992), conducted among patients referred to the Oxford NDU, involved 157 patients (84 in the 'treatment group') over 60 years of age originally admitted to hospital with a CVA, fractured neck of femur or for lower limb amputation. No significant difference was found between the groups in length of stay, although the treatment group stays were on average 4 days longer at 47 days. There was a statistically significant interaction between experimental group and diagnosis. Patients with fractured neck of femur had a shorter stay if in the control group whereas CVA patients in the treatment group had shorter stays than the CVA patients in the control group. Patients in the treatment group had significantly lower scores on a 'nursing dependence' index and higher levels of satisfaction with care. Interestingly, the mortality rates in the treatment group were significantly lower than the control group.

This study, although promising, has some weaknesses. The measures used were of questionable validity; in particular, the 'nursing dependence' index was completed through interview with the client as were the measures of life satisfaction and satisfaction with care. Pearson et al. (1992) noted problems with some of the scales and the need to adapt them to the particular circumstances. Perhaps of more concern is the fact that all measures were self-reported and hence all subject to the potential effect of response sets which were aimed at pleasing the investigator. This potential problem was noted by Pearson et al. (1992).

More recently Davies (1994) reported favourable outcomes on a nursing-led rehabilitation unit and Bradshaw (1995) described a similar service. However the evaluation of 'nursing beds' remains inconclusive. The best conclusion would be that the work of Pearson and his colleagues has demonstrated the feasibility of 'therapeutic nursing units' but much work remains to be done in consolidating knowledge as to the effectiveness of these units.

None of the studies which support the creation of 'therapeutic nursing units' fully distinguish between the three separate strands of the work of Pearson and his colleagues. The core hypothesis behind the development of the nursing-led service on Byron was that there existed a patient population whose primary need was nursing (Evans & Griffiths, 1994). The needs of these patients were such that their care could be managed by nurses without causing them harm. By grouping patients together in a single unit, the focus of nursing care for both these non-acute patients and those patients with acute medical conditions could be matched to patient need. This can reduce any conflicts in prioritising care and improve the chances of all patients receiving the appropriate care.

The unit was designed to impact upon the management of clinical care as a whole. Rather than testing to see if nursing has an impact on patient health outcomes, this was assumed to be so. The unit was designed to maximise the benefits (or minimise the harm) which nursing offers a particular patient group. Rather than testing the notion that therapeutic nursing can only be fully realised under certain circumstances, the work described here might be more reasonably described as the development of a clinical nursing speciality for a group of patients hitherto treated as in need of medical specialities. The descriptions given by Pearson and Kitson of 'therapeutic nursing' describe some of the mechanisms through which nursing may impact upon a patient's health. The specific relevance of these mechanisms to the notion of 'nursing units' or 'nursing-led care' remain largely untested.

# IMPLEMENTATION



## Background

Prior to the implementation of the nursing-led service on Byron Ward, the unit had operated as an acute medical ward dealing with patients covered by a variety of general medical consultants. Primary nursing had been practised on the unit for some time. Whereas there is considerable discussion surrounding the precise nature of 'primary nursing' and a variety of operational definitions are offered (Black, 1992; Bowman et al., 1991, 1993; MacGuire, 1989a, 1989b; Mead, 1991; Thomas & Bond, 1990), the common theme is that the delivery of nursing care is organised so that full accountability for the delivery of patient care is invested in the primary nurse (Evans, 1993).

In order for accountability for care to become a reality, certain preconditions must be met. The primary nurse must have the ability and knowledge to act within the given domain of responsibility. The primary nurse must have the authority to carry through action and, finally, there must be mechanisms through which the primary nurse can be called to account (Bergman, 1981; Evans, 1993). Although there is no fundamental difference between this concept of primary nursing and the role of the ward sister in a traditionally managed ward, the operationalisation passes the responsibility downwards to a level where those being held to account also have direct responsibility for delivering care to a caseload of patients with whom they are directly familiar. The primary nurse is given managerial responsibility for the team of nurses involved in delivering care to that group of patients (Evans, 1993).

This contrasts with other methods of organising care where the ward sister retains direct accountability and responsibility for care which is delivered to patients. Either a series of tasks may be allocated to nurses by the sister (Bowman et al., 1991; Thomas & Bond, 1990) or one of the variety of methods of team nursing may be deployed. In the case of team nursing, both responsibility and accountability are diffused below the level of ward sister who does not retain clear mechanisms through which to exercise her own responsibility or to hold others to account.

Although the notion of primary nursing is not synonymous with nurse-managed care or a 'nursing-led in-patient' unit, the experience of primary nursing prior to the development of the new service on Byron was an essential prerequisite for the service which has evolved. The fundamental logic of 'nurse-managed care' for patients whose nursing needs predominate is only sound if nursing is organised in such a way as to encompass both responsibility and accountability for all the care delivered to patients.

The operational descriptions offered here are crude descriptions of a model which was designed to maximise the benefit which patients accrue from their nursing care. The precise ways in which these mechanisms impinge upon nursing care and/or patients remain to be explored. Our earlier work (Evans & Griffiths, 1994) refers to the 17-bedded ward where the service was originally implemented from February to June 1993. As currently operated, and for the majority of the period described in this report, Byron operated as two distinct entities. Half of the ward was run as a traditional, medically-managed 'care of the elderly' ward for 11 patients with a single primary nursing team. This unit was geographically separate from the 'nursing-led' half of the ward which has 13 beds: eight on an open ward and five in individual cubicles. A single primary nursing team operates on this side of the ward. Unless specifically referring to the ward as a whole, references to 'Byron' should be taken to refer to the 'nursing-led in-patient service'.

## Patient progress through hospital

During the period described in this report, the service was offered to patients already in hospital on acute medical or care of the elderly wards. The original client group identified for the service was all patients with significant nursing

**FIGURE 1**

Patient journey through the hospital system

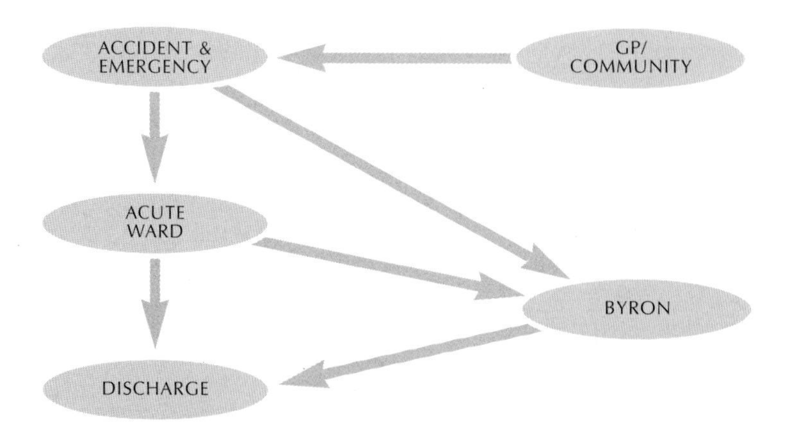

needs who had a need to remain in hospital after the resolution of acute medical crisis (Evans & Griffiths, 1994). Thus, rather than keeping patients in the acute area for the duration of the hospital stay, patients were transferred to Byron in order to focus upon the remaining problems and maximise function prior to discharge (FIGURE 1).

The entire patient stay (until discharge or referral to another clinical speciality) was recorded as a part of the same consultant episode. Although this was largely for administrative reasons, this mechanism serves to illustrate the continuing responsibility of the consultant – who retains the ultimate responsibility for the patient's medical care.

## Number of referrals

Data presented here are based upon referrals to Byron during the period February 1993 to September 1994. During this period a total of 168 referrals were received and followed up by unit staff. Excluded from the figures are a small number of patients who were referred explicitly for terminal care and a number who were transferred to the unit purely in order to await placement during periods of pressure on acute beds. No systematic data has been recorded on these patients although the numbers are small, representing at most an additional 10% to the figures presented. Also not recorded are patients who were rejected on the basis of information presented verbally to staff of the unit but for whom no written referral was ever received. There has been a considerable variation in the number of referrals received in any one month, with a maximum of 19 (in May 1993) and a minimum of three (in three different months). It is difficult to account for this variation. It appears that there may be a seasonal trend, with numbers of referrals dropping off over the summer months until late autumn, although this is speculative owing to the limited data available.

Staff involved in recruiting patients suggest other factors which may affect the fluctuations observed: changes in junior doctors (reducing referrals); pressure on acute beds (increasing referrals); the creation of a dedicated rehabilitation ward with extra therapy input for patients and the commensurate reduction in therapy input to Byron due to the withdrawal of the peripatetic rehabilitation team. Another major factor seems to be the anticipated availability of beds.

Patients are often referred when a prompt transfer can be arranged but not if delays are anticipated. This is believed to be the reason that significantly more women than men are referred to the service (which has more female beds) although a similar sex disparity has been noted in other units (Bradshaw, 1995; Pearson et al., 1992).

### Source of referrals

Referrals are made to the unit either from the multi-disciplinary discharge planning meetings held by all three medical firms, or direct from the medical team, usually following a consultant ward round. Of referrals, 49% (n = 83) come from the multi-disciplinary meetings, 51% (n = 86) from direct contact.

The range of patients referred to the unit is discussed in Chapter 3. However, it is important to note that initial judgement as to patient suitability is always dependent upon the decision of a member of the medical team to refer the patient. Thus the population of patients from which the unit draws its patients is largely defined by those referring patients to it. Although there appears to be a number of verbal referrals which are rejected by the unit staff as unsuitable at an early stage and therefore remain undocumented and unrecorded, it is unclear whether there are suitable patients who remain unreferred. The unit does not actively seek out potential patients on the wards, although clearly the discussion of a patient's condition at multi-disciplinary meetings allows the screening nurse to express an opinion on the potential suitability of patients not yet referred.

### In-patient stay prior to referral

Of patients, 79% (n = 132) were referred to the unit from acute medical wards with an additional 10% from care of the elderly wards (n = 17). About 5% (n = 8) were referred directly from the emergency admissions ward as they were in need of admission but did not require acute medical treatment. Other patients were referred to Byron from surgical (4%, n = 7) and other speciality wards (2%, n = 3) after completion of specialist treatment. During the period of this study, these patients could only be admitted to Byron if they had originally been admitted under a medical consultant. This is due to the fact that the beds of the nursing-led service in Byron remained part of the acute medical care group's bed allocation.

Mean length of hospital stay from admission to referral to Byron was 26 days, although there was a large variation with a range from 0 to 193 days in hospital prior to referral. Median time from admission to referral was 16 days, with 25% of patients referred within 6 days of admission.

It is interesting to note that the mean length of stay prior to admission to Byron seems to have fallen during the time period covered in this report, with very long lengths of stay before referral being the norm in the project's early months. However, some long delays in referring to Byron do not appear to be accounted for purely by fitness for transfer.

## Assessment

The operational guidelines originally developed for the unit envisaged that all referrals to the unit would receive a response within one working day. In all, 83% of referrals were assessed on the same day or the next, with a mean delay of 0.97 days (no allowance is made for weekends or bank holidays).

After receipt of a referral the patient is assessed by a member of the unit's team according to the unit's criteria (Evans & Griffiths, 1994). The assessment has two main purposes. First, the assessment is intended to ensure that there are no outstanding issues of medical care which could not be managed within the resources of the unit. The patient is physically assessed in order to ensure that there is a detailed baseline of the patient's physical well-being should the patient be transferred. This process of physical assessment is also intended to uncover problems which have emerged since the last detailed medical assessment. Second, the goals of transfer are identified and a judgement made of the potential for achieving these goals through nursing care and the available therapy resources.

The nature of the unit is described to the patient and/or their family and potential outcomes are explored. If the unit nurse determines that there is a reasonable expectation that the patient's outcomes would be improved by a period of nursing care on the unit, she arranges transfer. The planned treatment period on the unit would not normally exceed the currently planned period in the hospital system.

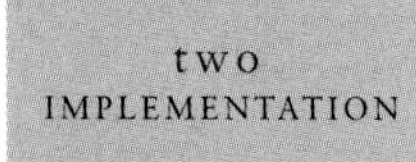


**TABLE 1**
Suitability for Byron

| SUITABILITY | N (%) |
|---|---|
| **Suitable at first assessment** | 118 (70.1) |
| **Suitable pending investigation** | 6 (3.6) |
| **Suitable pending other circumstances** | 10 (6.0) |
| **Suitable pending medical stability** | 29 (17.4) |
| **Unsuitable at first assessment** | 4 (2.4) |
| **Not fully assessed** | 1 (0.6) |

Few patients were deemed to be completely unsuitable for the unit at assessment (TABLE 1), although there may be considerable under-recording of patients who were deemed unsuitable on the basis of a verbal referral. A total of 70% (n = 118) of patients were assessed as being immediately suitable and only 3% (n = 5) were assessed as completely unsuitable. This high proportion of suitable patients may largely be due to the extremely open nature of the admission criteria. The main uncertainty relates to medical stability which leads to a rejection of 17% (n = 29) of patients at first assessment (although these patients may have been accepted for the unit pending medical stability). The judgement of suitability includes patients who are deemed suitable but are not accepted for the unit because a bed will not be available within the anticipated length of stay.

The proportion of suitable patients may be high because of the preselection of patients referred. These figures may simply reflect a high degree of consensus that certain patients are suitable. In addition, it is not known what proportion of potentially suitable candidates are referred to the service. The number of referrals is certainly considerably lower than that expected on the basis of pilot work for the unit. Some of the shortfall may be accounted for by parallel developments in rehabilitation services targeted at some of the potential client groups of the service.

## Transfer of patients

Once a patient has been accepted for the unit and all investigations completed (and condition stabilised if the patient was accepted pending medical stability), transfer is usually arranged into the next available bed. The operational plans for the unit had envisaged that the potential would exist to actively manage patient dependence, as it was anticipated that highly physically dependent patients would predominate. Although the latter expectation has been borne out, the level of referrals was such that actively managing the dependence mix by regulating admissions proved largely impossible. Occasionally patients with a shorter anticipated length of stay were transferred in preference to others in order to avoid discharge delays.

During the period May 1993 to September 1994, 76 patients were referred under the research protocol and transferred to Byron. For these patients, the mean delay from referral to transfer to Byron was 5.8 days. Given the large number of patients accepted pending stability, this figure is probably less meaningful (although more reliable) than the 'wait after readiness'. A patient was defined as ready either at the point that the assessment was completed if they were immediately ready or when the conditions for acceptance (i.e. completion of investigations, medical stability or obtaining consent) were met. The mean delay after this point was 2 days with 60% of patients (n = 46) being transferred on the day they were ready for transfer. All patients were transferred within 2 weeks of readiness.

## After transfer

After transfer, responsibility for managing care was delegated from the consultant to the primary nurse on Byron for as long as the patient remained medically stable. Although provision was made for dealing with non-acute, non-specialist medical problems within the unit, not all medical problems which might arise could be dealt with within the unit's resources. If such a problem arose, two options were available. A consultant physician could take over responsibility for care (as the balance of the patient's needs have shifted from nursing to medicine) but consider that the patient is still most appropriately nursed on Byron. Alternatively, the patient's needs may be such that they require transfer to an acute ward. Patients were managed without recourse to significant medical input in 82% (n = 62) of cases; 18% (n = 14) were accepted back under the care of a consultant physician for a period of their stay, with just over half of these remaining on Byron. In all, 8% of patients (n = 6) were transferred to acute wards for a period of their stay.

## Care on Byron

### Care management

Care is planned by the primary nurse with the support of the rest of the nursing team and is reviewed weekly at a multi-disciplinary care-planning meeting, which reviews patient goals and identifies strategies for achieving them. Representatives of all therapies are invited to attend the meeting, which is generally attended by social workers, a physiotherapist, an occupational therapist and nurses. Dieticians, pharmacists, and speech and language therapists attend if there are patients for whom they have considerable input or if there are particularly complex issues. Provision of occupational therapy services has been seriously affected by staff shortages throughout the period of the study and the unit has unfortunately been restricted to a home visit assessment service for periods of time.

The multi-disciplinary care-planning meeting is chaired by the screening/assessment nurse in order to facilitate the co-ordination of discharge planning activities and the admission of patients to the unit. In addition, a weekly meeting is held with the hospital's district nurse liaison/discharge planning co-ordinator in order to review and plan for community nursing needs. Case conferences are convened with relevant parties when necessary. In addition to this, there is a regular programme of case review between the ward manager or NDU leader and the primary nurse (Evans & Griffiths, 1994).

### Nursing assessment

Many aspects of nursing assessment have remained largely unchanged since the transition to nurse-managed care. Nursing care planning is conducted according to a format loosely based upon Roper et al. (1980) in common with most of the referring wards, although the actual form of the written plan differs from that used on other wards in the hospital. There is some evidence that care plans on Byron as a whole are more likely to be implemented and present a more comprehensive record of care delivered than on acute medical wards. It remains unclear whether this difference results from development work with the ward team, the change to nursing-led care, the documentation system itself or is an artefact of the case mix being skewed toward longer stay patients. The documentation system is the subject of a separate report currently being prepared.

In addition to the traditional care planning approach, an assessment framework has been designed specifically for use with the nursing-led patients. This framework is intended to document routine assessment for a wide range of physiological abnormalities. The intention of this framework is to facilitate a focused assessment in order to identify problems requiring medical intervention at the earliest possible stage (Evans & Griffiths, 1994).

## The nursing team

Staffing for the ward as a whole was calculated using the same formula as that for the acute medical wards at King's College Hospital. This resulted in a planned staffing of 2.5 nurses for the 13 patients on an early shift (7.45 a.m. – 3.15 p.m.), 2 on a late shift (1.45 p.m. – 9.45 p.m.) and 1.5 on a night shift (9.00 p.m. – 8.00 a.m.). The primary nursing team operating has varied over the period covered in this report; the current staffing is shown in Table 2.

**TABLE 2**
Current primary nursing team

| NUMBER OF STAFF | GRADE | TYPE |
|---|---|---|
| **1** | F | Primary nurse |
| **3** | E | Associate nurse |
| **4** | D | Associate nurse |
| **2** | A | Health-care assistant/nursing auxiliary |

All staff rotate onto night shifts; there are no permanent night staff. In addition, an F-grade nurse takes a co-ordinating role in assessing the suitability of patients for the unit, arranging transfer of patients and co-ordinating the discharge planning activities for patients on the unit.

The ward as a whole is managed by a G-grade ward manager who contributes three to four shifts per week (to the ward as a whole). The H-grade clinical leader contributes one or two clinical shifts (again to the ward as a whole) and provides support in areas such as case review and clinical advice, in addition to leading the unit's quality assurance and dissemination activities (Evans & Griffiths, 1994). The ward establishment also includes a research post which, in addition to taking lead responsibility for the research presented in this report, provides some input to the screening and assessment of patients, covering for annual leave, sickness and clinical shifts of the assessment nurse. A further post is funded from the ward establishment, that of a B-grade ward co-ordinator who provides administrative support to the clinical nursing staff of the whole ward: arranging transport, out-patient appointments, routine supply ordering and providing a first point of contact for enquiries to the ward.

As the planned configuration of the ward was to have a single smaller unit entirely comprising nurse-managed beds, all the original staff team participated in two 'away days' which were used to identify additional learning needs for staff involved in the new service. The main areas which were identified as needing additional input were specific skills (e.g. phlebotomy, cannulation, ECGs) and general skills in assessment, in particular physical assessment. As a result of needs identified, part of the unit's programme of staff development includes a rolling programme of attendance on a diploma-level course in assessment. Similarly, a rolling programme of staff attendance at courses in phlebotomy and cannulation is underway. Ward staff trained in assessment also run in-house courses for new staff in preparation for the formal course.

## The multi-disciplinary team

Although the patients referred to the unit are not deemed to be in need of acute medical services, they are in receipt of a range of therapy services. As it was evolving from an acute medical ward, it was planned that the unit would retain

TABLE 3

Therapy before & after transfer to Byron

| THERAPY | RECEIVING THERAPY BEFORE REFERRAL[a] N (%) | RECEIVING THERAPY ON BYRON N (%) |
|---|---|---|
| **Occupational therapy** | 54 (71) | 62 (84) |
| **Physiotherapy** | 65 (86) | 70 (91) |
| **Speech therapy** | 20 (26) | 18 (24) |
| **Rehabilitation**[b] | 11 (14) | 4 (5) |
| **Dietician** | 17 (22) | 25 (33) |
| **Social work** | 37 (49) | 57 (75) |
| **Pain team** | 6 (8) | 9 (12) |
| **All therapies** | 76 (100) | 76 (100) |

a Refers only to patients actually transferred to Byron, not all suitable patients. All data calculated from 76 patients transferred to Byron under the research protocol during the period May 93-Sept 94.

b Prior to the opening of the dedicated rehabilitation unit, the services of a peripatetic rehabilitation service were available to patients on Byron. After that time patients referred to Byron may also have been referred to that service but would not receive input if transferred to Byron.

the range and level of therapeutic inputs which were available to patients on acute medical wards.

For the period covered in this report, routine medical input has been provided on a sessional basis by a general practitioner, with emergency medical input from the existing hospital cover. This post is currently filled by a research registrar. The unit doctor attends for four 2-hour sessions per week. She attends to minor medical problems and provides advice and support in relation to liaising with and referring back for non-urgent specialist review. The majority of patients referred to Byron during the period of this report had been referred to, or were in receipt of, physiotherapy (86%, n = 65) and occupational therapy (71%, n = 54). There is also a significant level of input from other therapies

(TABLE 3). These figures include patients referred but not yet assessed but exclude patients no longer in receipt of a particular therapy.

It is difficult to assess whether the actual level of input from these services was the same as that offered to patients prior to transfer. In particular, despite the original provision for input to Byron equivalent to the acute medical wards, occupational therapy services to Byron were restricted at times during the period of this report. Service from other therapies remained at the approximate levels expected throughout the period and can be generally presumed to have met patient need throughout the period, although difficulty meeting the need for speech and language therapy of some patients has been noted by the therapists themselves at times. This has not affected Byron differentially.

Overall, patients on Byron receive input from significantly more members of the multi-disciplinary team than prior to their transfer [mean number of therapists: 2.76 before transfer compared with 3.24 on Byron. Wilcoxon signed-rank test of difference in location for two dependent groups (see Leach, 1979): z corrected for ties ($z_c$) = 2.98 $p < 0.01$]. Some of the difference could be attributed to purely 'structural' reasons. The reduced input from the rehabilitation team is a direct consequence of transfer to Byron. Conversely, input from social work is more likely to come at the end, rather than the beginning, of a hospital stay. Even after eliminating social work and the rehabilitation team from these figures, the difference remains significant (mean number of therapists: 2.13 before transfer compared with 2.43 on Byron. Wilcoxon signed-rank test $z_c = 2.98$ $p < 0.01$). The increased proportion of patients receiving input from other therapies is consistent across all therapies except speech therapy.

## Discharge

Discharge is planned by the primary nurse in close collaboration with the multi-disciplinary team, the patient and members of the patient's family. Stays on the unit have varied greatly, with a maximum length of stay of nearly 1 year and a minimum stay on the unit of 2 days. The median length of stay for all patients transferred to the unit was 41 days. Most patients are discharged to their own home. These issues are discussed in more detail in Chapter 4.

# PATIENT POPULATION



## Expectations

Preparatory work for the unit identified a range of patient groups who were liable to remain in hospital after the resolution of acute medical problems (Evans & Griffiths, 1994). The service was not targeted at particular diagnostic groups. Instead, core client groups were those in which nursing potentially played a major role in determining recovery and medicine a relatively minor or static one: e.g. a patient with an acute or chronic condition for which medical therapy has been optimised and whose condition has stabilised.

### Multiple problems

As can be seen from Table 4, multiple diagnoses are the norm with only 27% of patients (n = 26) having a single active diagnosis stated. The largest single grouping is of patients with three or more diagnoses. A total of 39% of patients transferred to Byron (n = 37) fell into this category.

The majority of patients were referred for a single reason (TABLE 4) whereas the Byron staff assessing suitability for transfer only identified a single reason in 37% (n = 36) of cases and identified three or more reasons for transfer in 40% (n = 38) of cases. Byron staff identified significantly more needs than those for which the patient was initially referred (Wilcoxon signed-rank test $z_c = -4.15$, $p < 0.01$). Byron nursing staff identified more needs than referrers in 25% (n = 24) of cases, identifying less in only 2% of cases (n = 2).

**TABLE 4**

Numbers of diagnoses and nursing needs for all patients transferred to Byron

| | NUMBER OF DIAGNOSES N (%) | NUMBER OF STATED REASONS FOR REFERRAL N (%) | NUMBER OF IDENTIFIED NEEDS N (%) |
|---|---|---|---|
| **1** | 26 (27) | 54 (56) | 36 (37) |
| **2** | 33 (34) | 15 (16) | 22 (23) |
| **3 or more** | 37 (39) | 27 (28) | 38 (40) |

## Reasons for referral and identified nursing needs

During pilot work, a taxonomy of nursing needs was developed. Referrers and assessing nurses were asked to use these categories to identify the reasons the patients were to be transferred to Byron (TABLE 5).

**TABLE 5**

Taxonomy of therapeutic nursing needs

| NEED CATEGORY | DEFINITION |
|---|---|
| **Education** | Patient or family need specific knowledge or skills, lack of which prevent safe discharge/cannot be taught after discharge |
| **Nurturing** | Patient requires non-specific caring in the in-patient environment in order to restore confidence/ability and enhance natural recovery; patient at risk of iatrogenic illness caused by or preventable by nursing |
| **Nutrition/feeding** | Patient has a remediable nutritional deficit and/or feeding difficulty |
| **Psychological** | Patient has (or is at risk of) a disturbance of mood due to disease or hospitalisation or has cognitive impairment which impairs function or mood |
| **Rehabilitation** | Patient suffers from self-care deficit due to mobility deficit which may be alleviated either through restoring mobility or improving function with disability |
| **Social problems** | Conditions exist which impair the patient's ability to return to their own home which operate independently of the physical/mental condition of the patient |
| **Symptom control** | Patient is suffering from a physical problem which is non-acute but where nursing intervention or assessment is required, e.g. continence control, bowel care, pain assessment |
| **TLC (tender loving care)** | Patient is in need of nursing care aimed at maintaining comfort during the terminal stage of a physical illness |
| **Wound care** | Patient has a wound which requires assessment, dressing and other intervention with a view to healing |

The profile of patients referred differed considerably from that anticipated. Education needs, nurturing and wound care were identified significantly more frequently in the pilot patient group than among actual referrals (TABLE 6). All categories were identified more frequently during pilot work than among the actual referrals, except for nutrition (13% anticipated, n = 6 compared with 15% actual, n = 14) and rehabilitation, which was identified as a need in 95% of patients. The category 'nurturing' was virtually unused. This may reflect the

**TABLE 6**

Nursing needs: comparison of actual with projected

| REFERRAL REASON | ACTUAL N (%) | PROJECTED N (%) | PROJECTED VERSUS ACTUAL (FISCHER'S EXACT TEST) |
|---|---|---|---|
| **Education** | 11 (12) | 24 (50) | Sc = 1680.5 z = 4.82 p < 0.01 |
| **Nurturing** | 1 (1) | 12 (25) | Sc = 1020.5 z = 4.38 p < 0.01 |
| **Nutrition/feeding** | 14 (15) | 6 (13) | Sc= 30.5 z = 0.11 p > 0.05 |
| **Psychological** | 15 (16) | 15 (31) | Sc = 633.5 z = 1.92 p > 0.05 |
| **Rehabilitation** | 90 (95) | 15 (31) | Sc = 2823.5 z = 7.89 p < 0.01 |
| **Social problems** | 10 (10) | 9 (19) | Sc = 303.5 z = 1.1 p > 0.05 |
| **Symptom control** | 10 (10) | 9 (19) | Sc = 303.5 z = 1.1 p > 0.05 |
| **Wound care** | 15 (15) | 31 (31) | Sc = 681.5 z = 2.09 p < 0.05 |
| **All reasons** | 95 (100) | 48 (100) | |

Sc = rank sum test statistic calculated according to the formula given by Leach, 1979. All Fischer's tests are performed using the normal approximation to S(z). S and the continuity correction are calculated according to the formula given by Leach, (1979).

Data from all patients transferred. N missing = 1.

fact that it is seen as a quality of nursing care as opposed to an intervention or need in itself.

It is unclear why there should be such a disparity in the needs identified. Although nurses from the unit agreed on the application of categories with considerable reliability, this cannot be expected to apply to those referring to the service. Their use of terms may in turn influence the assessment of need by Byron nurses. It may be that the near universal use of the category 'rehabilitation' by referrers influences assessing nurses who in turn do not identify more specific needs. If rehabilitation is used by referrers to categorise the needs of any patient needing further therapy to return to optimal functioning, it is likely to apply to nearly all of the patients referred to Byron. All categories of need other than rehabilitation were identified more frequently by nursing staff than referrers. In addition, the use of a check-list may have influenced the identification of categories, so that choice of one category influences the use (or non-use) of others, thus rendering the categories dependent on one another.

There may be a genuine perception on the part of referrers that the patients most likely to benefit from, or most suitable for, Byron are those with a remediable functional deficit. Although the disparity between actual referral patterns and the pilot work may be an artefact of the categorisation system, the higher than expected proportion of 'rehabilitation' needs among the patients on the unit is in accord with the impression of unit staff that the patient group which is being referred is skewed toward the more physically dependent, longer stay patients of the group identified as suitable in pilot work.

## Diagnoses

As with the identified needs and reason for referral, the diagnostic groups referred to the service differed considerably from those identified in pilot work (TABLE 7). Of particular note was the absence of diabetes as a primary diagnosis, the lower than expected number of patients with 'injury' and 'wounds' whereas 'CVA' and 'cardiac' were more frequent than expected, although none of these individual differences is statistically significant. 'Functional' diagnoses appeared as the main diagnosis significantly more frequently than expected.

**TABLE 7**

Main diagnoses: comparison of actual with projected

| DIAGNOSIS | ACTUAL N (%) | PROJECTED N (%) | PROJECTED VERSUS ACTUAL (FISCHER'S EXACT TEST) |
|---|---|---|---|
| **Cardiac** | 12 (13) | 3 (6) | Sc = 219.5<br>$z = 0.88$ $p > 0.05$ |
| **CVA** | 28 (29) | 9 (19) | Sc = 417.5<br>$z = 1.18$ $p > 0.05$ |
| **Diabetic** | 0 (0) | 3 (6) | Sc = 213.5<br>$z = 1.84$ $p > 0.05$ |
| **Functional** | 14 (15) | 0 (0) | Sc = 560<br>$z = 2.40$ $p < 0.05$ |
| **Gastrointestinal** | 3 (3) | 0 (0) | Sc = 65<br>$z = 0.58$ $p > 0.05$ |
| **Infection** | 10 (11) | 6 (13) | Sc = 18.5<br>$z = -0.07$ $p > 0.05$ |
| **Injury** | 16 (17) | 12 (25) | Sc = 300.5<br>$z = 0.95$ $p > 0.05$ |
| **Neurological** | 3 (3) | 3 (6) | Sc = 69.5<br>$z = 0.43$ $p > 0.05$ |
| **Other** | 6 (6) | 6 (13) | Sc = 230<br>$z = 1.06$ $p > 0.05$ |
| **Psychological** | 1 (1) | 0 (0) | Sc = –23.5<br>$z = -0.35$ $p > 0.05$ |
| **Wound** | 3 (3) | 6 (13) | Sc = 354.5<br>$z = 1.8$ $p > 0.05$ |
| **Total** | 95 (100) | 48 (100) | |

Analysing all diagnoses, more significant differences from the projected composition of the patient population emerge. Patients admitted to Byron were more likely to have a cardiac or functional diagnosis than projected whereas wound-related diagnoses were significantly less frequent than anticipated (TABLE 8).

Other categories demonstrated no significant difference in frequency from that anticipated. Despite the differences noted, the diagnoses which were expected to occur with some frequency did seem to do so. In particular, 'injury' and 'CVA', which between them were the main diagnoses in nearly 50% of the patient group admitted to Byron, were well represented.

The disparities which were noted between the anticipated client group and the actual one are interesting. The frequency of so-called 'functional' diagnoses is unexpected but consistent with the 'target' client group for the service of Byron. The large number of 'cardiac' patients possibly reflects the disabling nature of chronic cardiac conditions among the elderly and the sheer frequency of 'cardiac' diagnoses among the acute medical population in general.

The frequent appearance of the category 'functional' as the main reason for admission is noteworthy. Patients admitted following a fall were included in this category where the injury itself did not necessitate admission, as were patients with arthritic conditions. In itself this is unremarkable although it bears comment that the essential reason for admission (as opposed to out-patient investigation and treatment) could be defined in terms of nursing need (i.e. need for support in maintaining safety or in accomplishing activities of daily living) rather than their medical conditions. It was noted that frequently the reason cited for admitting a patient, or the event precipitating admission, was not a medical one. Whereas in some cases patients were admitted with 'falls' which clearly required investigation, in other cases the link between the loss of function and medical diagnosis was less obvious. In some cases, the diagnosis list included statements such as: 'Problems: 1, old CVA; 2, 'off legs', without a clear indication of any acute medical event (even after subsequent investigation). In other cases, there was a clear medical diagnosis such as urinary tract infection (UTI) but the problem list would contain secondary statements relating to a consequent loss of function, such as: 'Problems: 1, UTI; 2, 'off legs'.

**TABLE 8**

All diagnoses: comparison of actual with projected

| DIAGNOSIS | ACTUAL N (%) | PROJECTED N (%) | PROJECTED VERSUS ACTUAL (FISCHER'S EXACT TEST) |
|---|---|---|---|
| **Cardiac** | 22 (23) | 3 (6) | Sc = 699.5 $z = 2.27$ $p < 0.05$ |
| **CVA** | 30 (32) | 9 (19) | Sc = 228.5 $z = 0.62$ $p > 0.05$ |
| **Diabetic** | 10 (11) | 3 (6) | Sc = 303.5 $z = 1.10$ $p > 0.05$ |
| **Functional** | 28 (29) | 0 (0) | Sc = 702.5 $z = 2.04$ $p < 0.05$ |
| **Gastrointestinal** | 8 (8) | 0 (0) | Sc = 312.5 $z = 1.92$ $p > 0.05$ |
| **Infection** | 15 (16) | 6 (13) | Sc = 633.5 $z = 1.92$ $p > 0.05$ |
| **Injury** | 22 (23) | 12 (25) | Sc = 12.5 $z = 0.04$ $p > 0.05$ |
| **Neurological** | 4 (4) | 3 (6) | Sc = 21.5 $z = 0.12$ $p > 0.05$ |
| **Other** | 7 (7) | 6 (13) | Sc = 162.5 $z = 0.70$ $p > 0.05$ |
| **Psychological** | 10 (10) | 0 (0) | Sc = 123.5 $z = 0.53$ $p > 0.05$ |
| **Wound** | 3 (3) | 6 (13) | Sc = 588.5 $z = 2.01$ $p > 0.05$ |
| **Total** | 95 (100) | 48 (100) | |

The predominance of such secondary functional deficits is not surprising. It was this which in many cases represented the reason Byron was identified as being of potential benefit, as the patient was unable to return home until function was restored. Many of the patients falling into the category 'injury' were in fact in medical beds because of functional deficits. Some of these patients had been transferred to medical beds after orthopaedic surgery whereas others had relatively minor injuries which required admission because of the risk of further fall or other functional deficit rather than treatment of the injury itself.

Of more significance are the numbers of people admitted with a diagnosis which was identified (quite literally in a number of cases) as not coping, often written as 'acopia' in the medical record. It must be recognised that such deterioration in function is often the result of an underlying, undiagnosed pathology and the need for medical treatment should not be underestimated. Elderly patients with no medical diagnosis are identified as having a particularly poor prognosis when hospitalised (Maguire et al., 1986; Narain et al., 1988). However, the patients transferred to Byron had remained undiagnosed after investigation and hence can be assumed to have been admitted to an acute hospital without ever needing acute medical services.

### Summary

It was believed that although diagnosis would not define a patient's need for Byron, certain diagnostic groups would appear more frequently than others. Both preliminary surveys and the actual patient group confirmed that patients who have suffered a stroke and those on acute medical wards following some form of injury (including post-orthopaedic surgery) form core client groups for the service. Perhaps more surprising is the frequency of diagnoses relating to functional disorders, which would not in themselves require acute medical intervention, although this by no means precludes the need for medical assessment. Diagnoses in this category include not only patients admitted because of falls (as opposed to the resulting injury) but also a number of patients admitted for what appears to be a decline in functional status independent of any precipitating medical event.

A range of nursing needs were identified in pilot work, with education the most frequent, being identified in 50% of cases. However, both referring staff and Byron staff identified 'rehabilitation' as a need in 95% of cases actually referred, compared with 35% in pilot work. All need categories were identified less frequently than in pilot work except 'nutrition', which was identified as a need in 15% of cases. Wound care, symptom control and psychological care were each identified in 15% or less of patients by both referrers and Byron staff, although Byron staff identified significantly more needs than did referrers.

It is difficult to judge whether or not these differences, and those identified between the anticipated and actual diagnostic groups, account for a real difference in use of the service from that anticipated. What is clear is that the term 'rehabilitation' is used by both Byron staff and referring teams to identify the aim of transfer to Byron in the vast majority of cases.

CHAPTER four

# Clinical outcomes

## Measurement of clinical outcomes: a pilot research study

The results presented here are from a pilot study conducted from May 1993 to September 1994. The study was a quasi-experimental design. Patients referred to Byron were randomly allocated to the treatment group – where the intention was to transfer them to Byron if suitable – or a control group, who remained on medically managed wards (usually acute medical wards) for the duration of their hospital stay. More details of the design are given in Evans & Griffiths (1994) and a more detailed report on this pilot study is available from Byron. The sample comprised all patients referred to the service from acute medical or care of the elderly wards between May 1993 and September 1994 whom the assessment nurses of Byron considered potentially suitable (excluding those specifically referred for terminal care) and who consented to the research.

A total of 71 patients were assessed as suitable and agreed to participate in the study as members of the treatment group. Of these, 64 were transferred to Byron under nurse-managed care. All the 71 suitable patients form the treatment group. Inclusion in the treatment group of all those for whom there was an intention to treat (including those refusing the treatment) is recommended as a conservative strategy by Cook & Campbell (1979). A total of 48 patients were randomly allocated to the control group, having been assessed as suitable and willing to participate in the study. More patients were approached to participate in the study as members of the control group but refused to participate. This led to some differences in both size and composition of the groups.

## Hypotheses

The null hypotheses of the study are as follows:

Admission to the nursing-led ward will result in:

- net reduction in patient's length of stay in acute hospital beds
- no net increase in 'length of stay' from admission to hospital to full discharge to the community
- no difference in overall health status
- no differences in psychological well-being
- no differences in physical dependence
- no differences in dependence after discharge
- no difference in readmission rates
- no differences in nursing-related complications or mortality.

when compared with patients who are medically managed through the normal hospital system.

## Measurement

The selection of outcome measures (TABLE 9) is intended to give a broad evaluation of the patient's health status whilst focusing on those aspects which are generally expected to be sensitive to nursing care inputs (Naylor et al., 1991; Stewart & Archbold, 1992, 1993). In addition, due concern must be given to the abilities of a frail elderly population and their limited tolerance for repeated arduous examination (Bowsher et al., 1993).

**TABLE 9**

Outcome measures

Additional information was collected on age, sex, diagnoses and therapies received before and during the study period.

| OUTCOME | MEASURE |
|---|---|
| **Length of stay in acute hospital beds** | Days in hospital not on Byron |
| **Length of stay** | Total stay in hospital after referral to Byron |
| **Health status** | NHPD – 'health related distress' (McKenna et al., 1993) |
| **Psychological well-being** | GHQ 12 (Goldberg & Williams, 1988) |
| **Physical dependence** | Barthel index (Granger et al., 1979b; Mahoney & Barthel, 1965) |
| **Dependence after discharge** | Type of accommodation<br>Use of community services |
| **No difference in readmission rates** | Local readmissions retrieved from patient administration system |
| **Nursing-related complications** | Incidence of chest infection, UTI, pulmonary embolus, deep vein thrombosis, pressure sores during study period<br>Number of abnormalities on physical assessment |
| **Mortality** | In-patient mortality |

Patients were assessed by a member of Byron staff or the clinical researcher. A pre-test assessment was conducted as soon as practicable after referral to the service (mean delay < 1 day). Patients were then monitored throughout their hospital stay with a follow-up assessment to determine outcomes conducted within the 48 hours prior to discharge. All assessments were ward-based. All tests and assessments were performed twice. The first assessment occurred as soon as practicable after the patient was referred to Byron. The second as near as possible to the patient's discharge, but always within the 48 hours preceding discharge. The study period is defined from the date of initial assessment, although lengths of stay are recorded from the date of referral. These periods are chosen to ensure comparability between treatment and control group.

## Overview of results

A more detailed analysis of the data including details of the statistical tests is included as an appendix.

### Sample groups

Analysis of pre-test scores suggested that randomisation had not been completely successful in eliminating differences between the treatment and control groups. In particular, the control group were more physically dependent and were suffering from more complications at the time of referral. The main source of this difference appears to be a higher attrition rate from the control group in terms of refusal to participate in the study. Analysis of data from former control group patients suggests that inclusion of these patients would have moved the pre-test means closer together but would not have dramatically affected outcome measures. The groups appear to be equivalent in terms of their medical diagnoses, age and sex. No differences were noted between groups in the reasons they were referred to Byron or their identified nursing needs, with rehabilitation being the predominant reason for referring. Analysis of covariance (ANCOVA) was used to correct for difference in pre-test score between the groups where possible.

Both groups received the same level of input from professions other than medicine. Medical input to the treatment group was (unsurprisingly) dramatically reduced. However, of the patients transferred to Byron, 16% were referred back for a period of medically-managed care of whom half were transferred off the ward for a period of time.

### Length of stay

Overall mean length of stay in acute beds dramatically reduced (as expected) with estimates of the reduction ranging from a minimum saving of 35 days (assuming Byron has no effect on overall length of stay). The differences in length of stay from the point of referral to Byron are large. This difference was not significant when using the ANCOVA model to correct for pre-test differences. However, there is a suggestion from the data that the less physically dependent members of the treatment group may have shorter lengths of stay when compared with similar members of the control group. Adjusting for differences in Barthel scores gives an estimated length of stay for the treatment group of 47 days compared with 72 days in the control group for those patients who were discharged alive.

### Discharge destination

Members of the treatment group are significantly more likely to be discharged to their own home or sheltered accommodation than are the control group, who are more likely to be discharged to residential or nursing homes. Despite the higher proportion of discharges to independent living there is no difference in the level of community services provided or in readmission rates.

### Mortality rates

Mortality rates are similar between groups, although the rate in the treatment group is higher than the control group (18% versus 13%). This difference is not statistically significant. Some of the deaths from the treatment group occurred before transfer to Byron whereas others occurred after transfer on to other wards.

### Nurse-related complications

Patients in the treatment group are significantly less likely to be diagnosed as suffering from a chest infection or urinary tract infection during the study period. The incidence of pressure sores is also significantly lower in the treatment group. There also appears to be a large (and statistically significant) difference between groups in terms of abnormal assessment findings at discharge, even allowing for pre-test differences, with the treatment group demonstrating fewer abnormalities. These differences must be interpreted with caution as the technique of summing assessment scores has not been formally validated. In addition, it should be noted that the process which leads to diagnosis of chest infections or UTIs is different between the treatment group and the control group. It cannot be assumed that all occurrences are diagnosed or that all diagnoses are correct. It would be easier to interpret these data if they were reflected in the mortality rates.

## Health status and psychological well-being

The response to the two questionnaire-based measures was low, particularly in the control group. No differences emerged in the NHPD (general health status) while the GHQ (psychological well-being) demonstrated a significant difference between groups, with the control group experiencing more distress than the treatment group. Again, this should be interpreted with caution although it is difficult to imagine that happy members of the control group selected themselves out of the questionnaire systematically. The fact that the results from the two

**TABLE 10**
Statistical conclusions related to null hypotheses for the study

| NULL HYPOTHESIS | CONCLUSION | EFFECT OF BYRON ESTIMATED FROM THIS DATA |
|---|---|---|
| **Net reduction in patient's length of stay in acute hospital beds** | Supported | Reduced length of stay in acute beds |
| **No net increase in length of stay from admission to hospital to full discharge to the community** | Supported | Possible reduction in length of stay for patients with lower physical dependence |
| **No difference in overall health status** | Supported | None |
| **No differences in psychological well-being** | Not supported | Lower psychological distress |
| **No differences in physical dependence** | Supported | None |
| **No differences in dependence after discharge** | Not supported | Higher proportion discharged to own home/sheltered accommodation |
| **No difference in readmission rates** | Supported | None |
| **No difference in nursing-related complications** | Partially supported | Lower incidence of chest infection and pressure sores<br>Less abnormal assessment findings |
| **No difference in mortality** | Supported | None |

scales are different does suggest that the differences are not a product of attempts on the part of treatment group patients to please the investigator.

## Physical dependence

There were large differences between groups on Barthel index (physical dependence) at discharge. After adjusting for pre-test differences there was a 20-point difference (on a 100-point scale) between the groups, with the treatment group less dependent than the control. The more cautious analysis using ranked scores does not show this difference to be significant; however, applying the same analysis to raw scores does indicate a statistically significant difference.

Taken as a whole these data are encouraging (TABLE 10). However, caution must be applied. The involvement of the data collectors in the running of the unit introduces a possibility of bias. If it was assumed that bias was manifest by systematically selecting less dependent patients and recording the fact through the higher scores on the Barthel index, the ANCOVA model is almost certainly sufficient to make an adequate correction. The systematic recording of such differences does suggest that bias has not manifested itself directly in terms of bias in the rating. This fact is also confirmed by the consistency in differences obtained from nursing staff/direct observation of the patient (the Barthel index), 'hard' data such as length of stay and place of discharge, secondary data from the medical record and patient-completed questionnaires.

The randomisation protocol should eliminate the possibility of deliberate selection of patients with favourable outcomes, although bias can operate in subtle ways. In particular, the high rate of refusal to participate in the study from the control group is a cause for concern. Analysis of outcomes from members of the control group who refused to participate (and hence transferred to Byron) suggests that their inclusion would not have substantially altered the group differences (estimating their outcomes from their pre-test scores) and may have substantially increased them (estimating their outcomes from the actual outcomes of their stay on Byron). However, such an analysis is based on a number of estimates and assumptions. Factors operating outside the parameters of the statistical models applied cannot be fully corrected for.

# MOVING FORWARD

At the time of writing, plans are well advanced to expand the service offered by Byron to encompass all 23 beds on the unit, offering the service to a wider patient group. This might reasonably be seen as a time for the unit to sit back on its laurels and congratulate itself on success. Although it is true that the staff of the unit have accomplished much, it would be unwise to assume that the 'job' is finished.

## Clinical outcomes

The outcomes presented here certainly suggest that something may be different in what happens to patients when Byron is included in the model of hospital care. However, it would be wrong to argue from the results of the phase one study that the case is proven. The results are consistent with expectations and with the work of others, particularly that of Pearson et al. (1992) whose study the work here partly replicates.

There is a clear need to replicate the study with independent data collectors. Although it will probably never be possible to 'blind' the investigators from the experimental manipulation, it is possible to keep them more removed from the day-to-day planning and concerns of the unit than has happened to date. It is widely recognised in the social sciences that there is a danger of investigators 'going native'. There can be little doubt that in this case the investigators were natives. Although that position made it possible to conduct a fairly extensive study with limited resources, the potential for subjective bias cannot be ignored. The analyses presented illustrate that there are limits on how far these results might be biased and have explored and corrected for such bias where possible. However, the best way of dealing with bias is to attempt to remove it.

The unit has secured funding in order to extend and replicate the phase one study. The next stage of the study will commence in April–May 1995. Data will be collected by independent researchers employed through King's College, University of London. The study will also be extended in order to explore outcomes in the longer term, rather than just within the hospital system.

One vital aspect of this study will be to refine our understanding of what actually happens to patients while they are on Byron. Although the formal processes are described here, it leaves the bulk of the activity called 'nursing care' largely unexamined. Assuming that the differences detected here are real differences, we cannot yet describe the precise mechanisms through which they were achieved beyond the mechanisms envisaged in the research hypotheses.

## Intermediate care

The concept of 'intermediate care' is increasingly seen as a solution to some of the problems facing the modern NHS and in particular the interface between acute and primary care services in London (Audit Commission, 1992; Department of Health, 1993; King's Fund Institute, 1994; Russel et al., 1994; Department of Health, 1994).

However, there are a range of models appropriate to different people at different points in their life and their 'career' as a patient. Marks (1994) suggests that the case for high technology care at home (hospital at home) is most clearly demonstrated in cases where there is no multiple pathology, where there is an element of non-professional help and where training is not too complex. Given the nature of the community served by King's Healthcare (deprived inner city) and the patient population served by Byron Ward to date (largely elderly and with mixed pathology) the development and evaluation of alternatives to hospital at home for this client group is crucial. There is a clear need to explore the boundaries between hospital and community for these patients and to develop further the links which the unit has with community providers.

Another key element of the potential for the model offered by Byron for intermediate care is its cost. Work has so far proceeded on the assumption that the unit is cost-neutral in terms of nursing staff as the formula used to determine nursing staff levels was the same across all units involved in the study. Phase two of the evaluation will include a more comprehensive economic analysis conducted by the York Centre for Health Economics.

## Teamwork

The work completed so far would not have been possible without the support (and considerable forbearance) of colleagues in a number of disciplines. However, if this report has created an impression of universal harmony and support for the work of Byron it would be unfair. Rightly, Byron has much to prove.

A series of interviews were conducted by the project development nurse during 1993 (the first year of operation) in order to clarify the views of the service held by other disciplines. This produced an interesting range of views. Although respondents were generally positive about Byron and often articulated the need for the service very clearly, they also identified problems.

One physiotherapist identified the suitable patients as:

*'patients that I do treat but I don't have that much time for or who are low priority by standards on an acute ward, who just need more time, who are just left sitting by their bed most of the day...people who are sort of waiting and not really getting anywhere because they need a little bit more help to get home, particularly on acute wards where maybe therapy staff and nursing staff are generally more stretched.'*

This view is clearly congruent with the aims of the unit.

However, she also identified a general lack of information concerning the unit saying that there was:

*'probably not enough information on it or we haven't been told enough about it, there's a lot of misconceptions'.*

Another respondent identified the practical consequences of communication difficulties:

*'I had about two or three patients...and they got transferred down sort of halfway through their care from speech therapy and it wasn't very well co-ordinated in that we didn't know if the patients were going so it was some days 'til we could get the notes down.'*

The comments of a doctor who worked on Byron in the capacity of an on-call emergency resource for the nursing patients, in addition to working on the consultant-managed half of the ward, is instructive. The positive aspects of nursing on Byron are clearly acknowledged saying that the nurses:

*'take initiative and responsibility....you're not hiding behind anybody.'*

Another was appreciative of the assessment skills deployed by nurses on Byron when calling for medical assistance:

*'they will usually have done a brief assessment... might have thought about sending some initial blood tests off, sometimes these will have been done... they've got more confidence. They'll look at the patient as a whole and see whether they're symptomatic, whether they've got headaches or whatever in the case of high blood pressure so they'll be less alarmist...'*

Asked what the patients got on Byron that was different, the response of an occupational therapist was:

*'Someone sitting down to talk to them. You see it because they always say to you afterwards 'I've discussed it with my nurse or X (primary nurse) says this.'*

However, this highlights a problem. The same occupational therapist felt that this could cause conflict when opinions differed, particularly because there was then a need to:

*'convince them (the patient) because they trust that person more (the nurse).'*

This highlights the potential for conflict which arises when interdisciplinary boundaries are perceived as being crossed. There is a widespread perception that Byron does not work in a multi-disciplinary fashion. One doctor saw it as nurses taking:

*'a more complete role... rather than simply play the nursing role.'*

Byron is perceived as:

*'more reluctant to get other teams involved... physiotherapy..., occupational therapy.'*

In many ways this appears to be the price paid for a nursing-led initiative. Despite the fact that patients on Byron are just as likely to get input from the multi-disciplinary team than comparable patients on other wards, the impression remains that they do not.

Some of the source of this conflict can be deduced from an examination of what the nursing role is perceived as being. A doctor summarised it thus:

*'making sure the patients are getting their medicines on time, that they get their observations done, that all their pressure areas are intact, that they are kept*

*clean and warm, fed and to check that their treatment is progressing as it should and that they're not regressing in any way.'*

This contrasts with the occupational therapist's role of 'assessing the activities of daily living' and the physiotherapist 'mobilising'. Although not disputing the role of physiotherapists in mobility or the role of occupational therapist in functional assessment, the idea that nursing's involvement in these areas might be perceived as an extended role would come as something of a surprise to most practising nurses, although this view is entirely consistent with the traditional medical model of care. Physiotherapists and occupational therapists may not be entirely comfortable with the boundaries set for their own professions.

## Byron as a rehabilitation ward

The unit operates in a changing world. When the unit was originally conceived there were no dedicated rehabilitation wards within the hospitals from which Byron draws its patients. Instead, rehabilitation was seen as a part of the work on all wards. Although Byron did not see itself as a rehabilitation ward, it is clear that many of the people referring patients to it did. Rehabilitation became a convenient catch-all term for the needs of the client group. There are now alternative client rehabilitation services with more or less clearly defined client groups. It is vital that the service finds a way of articulating its distinct contribution within that changing environment.

The data presented here strongly suggest that Byron may have a positive contribution to make to the care of some patients. The data may also go some way to describing the client group more closely. However, the dimensions used (medical diagnosis, health status and physical dependence) clearly fail to describe the essence of the need for many of these patients. Much work must be done in order to clarify further who Byron is for. It may be that the way forward lies in comparing the outcomes of patients managed through Byron directly with those managed through alternative rehabilitation services in order to further our understanding of who benefits most from the range of rehabilitation services on offer to patients.

## Acceptability

No formal work has been conducted on patient satisfaction in relation to Byron. The reasons for this are numerous. The concept of patient satisfaction is an elusive one, as can be seen in discussions such as that offered by Bond & Thomas (1992) or Fitzpatrick (1990). The decision to omit formal measurement of the concept from this study was based on the fact that the meaning of the concept was unclear in the current context. In particular, the approach to patient satisfaction taken in the Oxford study the 'Patient Services Checklist' (Pearson, 1987, 1992; Pearson et al., 1992) was seen as irrelevant to the intervention being evaluated. Any scale which specifically focuses on the activities of health-care professions within their traditional roles is largely irrelevant when evaluating a health-care system which changes those roles. Thus, although there is no dispute that a patient's answer to items such as 'Had to wait too long for a bedpan' from the patient services checklist (Pearson, 1987) is of crucial importance in evaluating the quality of nursing care, the answer says little about the innovation under consideration. Questions from more general satisfaction indices relating to the quality of interaction with doctors become confusing in the context of a unit in which nursing-led care is the norm and routine medical input is minimised.

The very low rate of refusal to transfer to the unit suggests that the idea of nurse-managed care is acceptable to patients and their families. The relatively low levels of psychological distress detected among patients on the unit may be taken as an indication that the unit does not induce undue distress. Anecdotally, a conversation with one former patient who, when asked how she felt about being on a nurse-managed unit, replied to the effect that she couldn't really see any difference: 'I get to see the doctors when I need to but they don't come round and bother me when I don't' says a lot about the acceptability. Whereas nurses may wish to hear eloquent descriptions from patients extolling the virtues of therapeutic nursing, such simple statements perhaps make the point more forcefully. Patients do not appear to mind. The benefits which may accrue in terms of clinical outcomes are unlikely to be noticed by patients because they largely relate to events which don't happen. A successful outcome is one where the patient doesn't get a pressure sore, doesn't stay in hospital longer than necessary or doesn't fail to regain independence.

## Conclusion

This report gives a cautiously optimistic view of the success of Byron. The next few years will show if the initiative can stand the test of time. The development of the unit within the mainstream clinical service has ensured that the unit has had to face the harsh realities of life in the modern NHS many times already and has shown that, although not perfect, the service is flexible enough to survive in the short term.

The work of Byron is significant to the development of nursing as a profession, providing an arena where the reality of autonomous practice can be faced and the benefits for the practitioner can be realised. However, the purpose of the innovation was to improve patient care. The results of the study are tantalising. They cannot be said to prove the benefits with any certainty, and the need to extend and replicate the pilot study is obvious. On the other hand, there is little doubt that the group of patients who were managed on Byron were more likely to return to independent living, were more physically able when they did so and experienced fewer complications while they were in hospital. The question which remains to be answered is 'why?'

# Analysis and results of pilot study

## Pre-test

### Pre-test scores

An analysis of the pre-test scores identified some pre-test differences between the two groups, not unexpected given the large number of pre-test comparisons (Table 11). However the differences are of substantive relevance to the research questions.

**TABLE 11**

Pre-test comparisons between treatment and control groups

| VARIABLE | PRE-TEST GROUP DIFFERENCE | DIRECTION |
|---|---|---|
| **Age** | No | |
| **Length of stay before referral** | No | |
| **Sex** | No | |
| **NHPD** | No | |
| **GHQ** | No | |
| **Physical assessment** | Yes | Higher score in control (i.e. more abnormalities) |
| **Physical dependence** | Yes | Higher score in treatment (i.e. less dependent) |
| **Level of dependence at prior accommodation** | No | |
| **Type of community service** | No | |
| **Number of community services** | No | |
| **Type of diagnosis** | No | |
| **Number of diagnoses** | No | |

Of the study population, 75% were female with a mean age of 77 years. They had been in hospital for a mean of 23 days prior to referral. There were no significant differences between treatment (T) and control (C) groups. No group differences were noted in health-related distress or psychological well-being. The mean score on the NHPD was 8.8 (T) and 7.8 (C) [range of possible scores 0–24 with a high score indicating a high level of health-related distress, Mann–Whitney $U = 301$, $z_c = -0.57$, $p > 0.05$, $n = 19$ (C) and 35 (T)]. No significant difference was detected in psychological distress by the GHQ-12, with means of 4.8 (T) and 3.1 (C) [range of possible scores 0–12 with 12 indicating a high level of distress, Mann–Whitney $U = 192$, $z_c = -1.81$, $p > 0.05$, $n = 16$ (C) and 35 (T)].

There was a significant difference in the summed physical assessment scores between the groups, with the control group demonstrating more physical symptoms and abnormalities (Mann–Whitney $U = 1184$, $z_c = -2.51$, $p < 0.05$). The mean number of abnormalities was 5.9, median 5 (T) and 8.1, median 7.5 (C). The control group was significantly more physically dependent at pre-test than the treatment group. Mean Barthel score was 46.13, median 40 (T) and 36.35, median 32.5 (C); the range of scores for the Barthel index was 0 (complete dependence) to 100 (independence) (Mann–Whitney $U = 1300$, $z_c = -2.19$, $p < 0.05$). The location of the different means for the two groups is of considerable interest as a score of 40 is the demarcation point between 'marked' dependence and 'severe' dependence (Granger et al., 1979a). An independent means t-test (i.e. test for difference in location of means) is also significant ($t = -2.14$, $df = 117$, $p < 0.05$), although the confidence intervals for the difference do include values above 40 for the mean of C.

**TABLE 12** Type of accommodation before admission

| | GROUP | | |
|---|---|---|---|
| ACCOMMODATION | TREATMENT N (%) | CONTROL N (%) | TOTAL N (%) |
| **Own home** | 62 (87) | 40 (83.3) | 102 (85.7) |
| **Sheltered accommodation** | 7 (9.9) | 1 (2.1) | 8 (6.7) |
| **Residential home** | 1 (1.4) | 5 (10.4) | 6 (5) |
| **Nursing home** | 1 (1.4) | 2 (4.2) | 3 (2.5) |

Whereas there was no difference in overall level of dependence for accommodation (TABLE 12), specific differences do appear to be present. More patients in the treatment group were admitted from sheltered accommodation than the control group. More control group patients were admitted from residential and nursing homes.

For those patients who were living in accommodation other than nursing homes, all health and social services which they received were recorded and the total number summed. There are no significant differences in the number of services or between groups in the number of diagnoses (Mann–Whitney U = 1630.5, $z_c = -0.43$, $p > .05$: mean for T = 1.83, median 2, mean for C = 1.77, median 2) or the type of diagnosis (TABLE 13).

No difference was detected in terms of receipt of other therapies. Both groups received the same number of therapy inputs (Mann–Whitney U = 1575, $z_c = -0.526$, $p > 0.05$, mean for T = 2.6, median 3, mean for C = 2.8 , median 3). The lack of any differences are surprising given the group differences noted in physical dependence and abnormalities on physical assessment. One possible explanation is that the groups are largely identical except that the control group differs on a single latent variable of 'illness'. Thus we would not expect to see differences in diagnoses or need for therapeutic input.

## Implication of pre-test group differences

Given the large number of significance tests, it is important not to overemphasise the 'significance' of two statistically significant differences between the treatment and control groups. However, the two dimensions on which the groups differ are of crucial importance to the nature of the experimental hypothesis and thus bear some discussion before progressing to an analysis of the post-test scores.

The choice of an analysis of covariance (ANCOVA) approach to data analysis was predicated upon a recognition that there would be a need to adjust an individual's outcome measures, depending upon individual differences at pre-test. All tests of significance for the treatment effect are effectively corrected for the group differences in pre-test scores. Whereas this procedure is not unproblematic in terms of its ability to provide estimates of treatment effects (Cook & Campbell, 1979), it must be remembered that the allocation to groups was

**TABLE 13**

Frequency of occurrence of all diagnoses in experimental and control groups

| DIAGNOSIS | GROUP<br>TREATMENT N (%) | CONTROL N (%) | ALL N (%) | FISCHER'S EXACT TEST[a] |
|---|---|---|---|---|
| **Cardiac** | 17 (24) | 12 (25) | 29 (24) | Sc = –23.5 z = –0.09 p > 0.05 |
| **CVA** | 24 (34) | 23 (48) | 47 (40) | Sc = 421.5 z = 1.35 p > 0.05 |
| **Diabetic** | 7 (10) | 4 (8) | 11 (9) | Sc = –7.5 z = –0.04 p > 0.05 |
| **Functional** | 23 (32) | 10 (21) | 33 (27) | Sc = 334.5 z = 1.17 p > 0.05 |
| **Gastrointestinal** | 4 (6) | 2 (4) | 6 (5) | Sc = –9.5 z = 0.07 p > 0.05 |
| **Infection** | 11 (15) | 11 (23) | 22 (18) | Sc = 193.5 z = 0.78 p > 0.05 |
| **Injury** | 16 (23) | 8 (17) | 24 (20) | Sc = 140.5 z = 0.55 p > 0.05 |
| **Neurological** | 2 (3) | 6 (12) | 8 (7) | Sc = 270.5 z = 1.69 p > 0.05 |
| **Other** | 4 (6) | 3 (6) | 7 (6) | Sc = –38.5 z = –0.26 p > 0.05 |
| **Psychological** | 11 (15) | 3 (6) | 14 (12) | Sc = 140.5 z = 0.26 p > 0.05 |
| **Wound** | 6 (8) | 4 (8) | 10 (8) | Sc = 255.5 z = 1.24 p > 0.05 |
| **Total** | 71 (100) | 48 (100) | 119 (100) | |

a All Fischer's tests are performed using the normal approximation to S(z).

initially random. The main potential source for non-random effect is the differential attrition noted from the control group.

## Outcomes

The primary significance testing for all ANCOVAs was performed using ranked data rather than raw scores. Whereas the disadvantage lies in the loss of information concerning the difference between (and within) subjects, the use of ranked data protects against violations of regression assumptions by treating ordinal data as interval and, more importantly, reduces the influence of extreme values. Although the tests are less sensitive, it is reasonable to apply a cautious approach to the interpretation of these data.

All the main ANCOVA analyses presented in this report were subjected to careful scrutiny in order to detect the signs of major violations of the assumptions made for regression analysis, of which ANCOVA procedures can be regarded as a subset. The procedures applied are described in Everitt & Dunn (1983, p.143–148). Graphical analysis of residuals give no indication that regression assumptions are violated when applying the ANCOVA model to the ranked data.

## Length of hospital stay

Mean length of stay in hospital from time of referral is considerably shorter for the treatment group, with a difference in means of 24 days and a median difference of 18 days (TABLE 14). Clearly, no equivalent figure exists for length of stay on Byron as there is no defining point when transfer occurs. The mean length of stay from referral for the treatment group is 45 days and the control group 69 days.

**TABLE 14**

Length of stay after referral to Byron

| GROUP | N | MEAN (DAYS) | MEDIAN (DAYS) | TRIMMED MEAN[a] (DAYS) | MINIMUM (DAYS) | MAXIMUM (DAYS) | STANDARD DEVIATION |
|---|---|---|---|---|---|---|---|
| **Treatment** | 71 | 45 | 36 | 43 | 1 | 138 | 32.33 |
| **Control** | 48 | 69 | 54 | 65 | 4 | 228 | 58.89 |
| **Length of stay on Byron** | 64 | 44 | 35 | 42 | 2 | 137 | 28.92 |

a 5% trimmed mean calculated by the minitab 'describe' command (Minitab, 1991) which is calculated after removing the highest and lowest 5% of values.

The Barthel score at pre-assessment has the strongest (and statistically significant) relationship of any of the pre-test scores with length of stay from referral. As this is both a theoretically hypothesised predictor of length of stay (Maguire et al., 1986; Narain et al., 1988) and the only numerical pre-test measure which significantly correlates with length of stay from referral, this was included as a covariate in the ANCOVA.

Unlike other aspects of the outcome of hospital stay, the meaning of any hospital stay is ambiguous in the extreme. In particular, any length of stay, whether short or long, clearly does not have the same implications if the patient dies in hospital. Removing from the analysis those patients who died leaves a total of 100 (58 in group T, 42 in group C; FIGURE 2).

| Source | df | Seq SS | Adj SS | Adj MS | F | p |
|---|---|---|---|---|---|---|
| Group | 1 | 3404.9 | 649.7 | 649.7 | 0.90 | 0.346 |
| Barthel | 1 | 7600.6 | 6476.1 | 6476.1 | 8.92 | 0.004 |
| Group x Barthel | 1 | 2620.2 | 2620.2 | 2620.2 | 3.61 | 0.060 |
| Error | 96 | 69672.8 | 69672.8 | 725.8 | | |
| Total | 99 | 83298.5 | | | | |

**FIGURE 2**

Annotated minitab output from general linear model analysis: ANCOVA on length of stay. ref, referral; seq, sequential; SS, sum of squares; MS, mean square; adj, adjusted.

Analysis of covariance for length of stay from referral without patients who died.

Test of model length of stay from ref = group + Barthel + group x Barthel.

There is no significant effect of group on length of stay (FIGURE 2), although the interaction effect is near statistical significance ($p = 0.06$). The estimates given from the raw data for this model give an adjusted mean length of stay for the treatment group of 47 days whereas that of the control group is 72. This suggests that the deaths in the control group are tending to occur at an earlier point in the stay and thus lower the figures for length of stay in that group.

It is of particular interest that the interaction term in this model (the raw data version) is significant, indicating that the regression slopes are not actually parallel. Thus these data suggest that the intervention of Byron has little effect on length of stay for patients who are highly dependent, who tend to have long lengths of stay regardless of intervention, whereas less physically dependent patients may benefit from the intervention.

The interaction effect must be treated with caution as the treatment group includes patients who are not transferred to Byron due to a short anticipated length of stay. The estimates of length of stay from referral provided by the application of the same statistical model to the data including only those members of the treatment group actually transferred gives an adjusted length of stay of 49 days for the treatment group and 63 days for the control group.

It is worth considering the implication of attrition from the control group. It is difficult to estimate 'what if' for this group of patients as they were transferred to Byron, but a reasonable approach seems to be to apply the regression equation derived from the ANCOVA on the raw data to the pre-test data from these patients. Nine members of the control group who refused to take part, allowed data to be recorded. All these patients were transferred to Byron. Applying the regression equation derived from the raw data analysis of covariance, the mean predicted length of stay for these nine patients would be 54 days. If this length of stay actually occurred it would move the adjusted means for the control group towards that of the treatment group but the gap would still be large. In fact, the actual mean length of stay from referral for these patients was 90 days, suggesting the operation of a separate factor not accounted for in the model.

In order to estimate the length of time in acute beds saved by transfer to Byron, the same statistical model (i.e. adjusting for physical dependence) was applied to the overall length of stay less time spent on Byron. An adjustment was included for those patients who were transferred back from Byron to other wards. The length of stay on Byron was estimated to be reduced by 50% in these cases (almost certainly an overestimate). The mean length of stay in acute beds was 27 days for the treatment group compared with 98 days for the control group (TABLE 15).

**TABLE 15**
Length of stay in acute beds

| GROUP | N | MEAN (DAYS) | MEDIAN (DAYS) | TRIMMED MEAN (DAYS) | MINIMUM (DAYS) | MAXIMUM (DAYS) | STANDARD DEVIATION |
|---|---|---|---|---|---|---|---|
| **Treatment** | 71 | 27 | 19 | 24 | 3 | 98 | 25 |
| **Control** | 48 | 98 | 76 | 91 | 11 | 341 | 74 |

A two sample t-test reveals this difference to be statistically significant (unsurprisingly) and provides a 95% confidence interval for the difference ranging from 49 days to 93 days ($T = -6.42$, $df = 54$, $p < 0.01$). If the estimate is based purely on reduction in length of stay in acute beds for patients transferred to Byron with no reference to the control group, the same adjustment for periods outside Byron gives a mean stay on Byron of 42 days. The 95% confidence interval for this mean ranges from 35 to 49 days. This estimate is based on the assumption that transfer to Byron makes no overall impact on length of stay.

## Place of discharge

Given that admission from a residential home or nursing home virtually determines readmission to a similar establishment, such patients are omitted from this analysis.

**TABLE 16**

Place of discharge

| | GROUP | | |
|---|---|---|---|
| PLACE OF DISCHARGE | TREATMENT N (%) | CONTROL N (%) | ALL N (%) |
| **Other NHS** | 2 (4) | 2 (5) | 4 (4) |
| **Nursing home** | 5 (9) | 14 (37) | 19 (20) |
| **Residential** | 5 (9) | 4 (11) | 9 (10) |
| **Sheltered** | 3 (5) | 2 (5) | 5 (5) |
| **Own home** | 41 (73) | 16 (42) | 57 (61) |
| **Column total** | 56 (100) | 38 (100) | 94[a] (100) |

a All live discharges not admitted from nursing home or residential home.

The difference between groups is significant ( = 12.55, df = 4, $p < 0.01$). The difference is almost entirely attributable to the far higher proportion of patients discharged home from Byron (73%) compared with the control group (42%) (Fischer's exact test on proportion returning to own home versus other, Sc = 615, $z = 2.8$, $p < 0.01$). This difference remains significant if sheltered accommodation is included in the category 'own home' (Fischer's exact test, Sc = 525, $z = 2.58$, $p < 0.01$).

There is no significant difference in the number of community services received after discharge. Eliminating patients discharged to nursing homes or other NHS facilities, the treatment group received a mean of 1.9 services and the control group 2.5 (Mann–Whitney U = 498.5, $z_c = -0.945$, $p > 0.05$). There is no significant difference in the utilisation of any individual service between groups (TABLE 17). The significantly higher proportion of patients discharged home from the treatment group must therefore be accounted for by some factor other than increased community service utilisation.

**TABLE 17**

Community health and social services received by patients not discharged to nursing home

| SERVICE RECEIVED | GROUP TREATMENT N (%) | CONTROL N (%) | ALL N (%) | FISCHER'S EXACT TEST |
|---|---|---|---|---|
| **Day centre** | 3 (6) | 2 (8) | 5 (7) | Sc = -12 z = –0.16 p > 0.05 |
| **Day hospital** | 3 (6) | 3 (12) | 6 (8) | Sc = 36 z = 0.45 p > 0.05 |
| **District nurse** | 23 (48) | 15 (63) | 38 (53) | Sc = 132 z = 0.91 p > 0.05 |
| **Home help** | 20 (42) | 14 (58) | 34 (47) | Sc = 156 z = 1.08 p > 0.05 |
| **Meals on Wheels** | 16 (33) | 11 (33) | 27 (37) | Sc = 108 z = 0.77 p > 0.05 |
| **Occupational therapy** | 3 (8) | 2 (6) | 5 (7) | Sc = 12 z = –0.16 p>0.05 |
| **Others** | 7 (29) | 10 (21) | 17 (24) | Sc = 60 z = 0.49 p > 0.05 |
| **Physiotherapy** | 4 (8) | 1 (4) | 5 (7) | Sc = 12 z = 0.16 p > 0.05 |
| **Social worker** | 8 (17) | 3 (13) | 11 (15) | Sc = 12 z = –0.12 p > 0.05 |
| **Column total** | 48 (100) | 24 (100) | 72 (100) | |

The readmission rate is similar in both groups (TABLE 18) although final collection of readmission data has not yet been completed (readmission data was collected from the patient administration system after the last patient was discharged; 28-day readmission rates are correct, whereas longer-term rates remain to be finalised). There are no significant differences in readmissions for any of the periods examined. Overall readmission rates are almost identical (21% T versus 19% C) with remarkably few early readmissions. Only 4% of patients were readmitted within 4 weeks, two from each group.

**TABLE 18**
Readmission for treatment and control group patients

| | GROUP | | | |
|---|---|---|---|---|
| TIME PERIOD FOR READMISSION | TREATMENT N (%) | CONTROL N (%) | ALL N (%) | FISCHER'S EXACT TEST |
| **Within 1 week** | 0 (0) | 1 (2) | 1 (1) | |
| **Within 2 weeks** | 1 (2) | 2 (5) | 3 (4) | |
| **Within 3 weeks** | 1 (2) | 2 (5) | 3 (4) | |
| **Within 4 weeks** | 2 (3) | 2 (5) | 4 (4) | Sc = –18 z = –0.19 p > 0.05 |
| **Within 60 days** | 6 (10) | 3 (7) | 9 (9) | Sc = 28 z = 0.2 p > 0.05 |
| **Within 90 days** | 7 (12) | 4 (10) | 11 (11) | Sc = 12 z = 0.08 p > 0.05 |
| **Within 120 days** | 8 (14) | 4 (10) | 12 (12) | Sc = 54 z = 0.33 p > 0.05 |
| **All readmissions** | 12 (21) | 8 (19) | 20 (20) | Sc = -10 z = –0.05 p > 0.05 |
| **Never readmitted** | 46 (79) | 34 (81) | 80 (80) | |

No determination has been made of reason for admission, although clinical speciality was identified. As all readmissions within 28 days were to acute medical specialities, it is reasonable to assume that these are all unplanned readmissions. It must also be noted that the figures do not include readmissions to other hospitals.

If readmissions from home are examined in isolation, the situation is little changed. A total of 44 patients from the treatment group and 18 from the control group were discharged to their own home or sheltered accommodation. Both groups have a readmission rate of 5% within 28 days (2 treatment, 1 control) with an overall rate of 20% (21% treatment, n = 12; 20% control, n = 5).

## Mortality

The mortality rates found in the experimental groups are broadly comparable with the findings identified during the evaluation of the Oxford 'nursing beds' (Pearson et al., 1992). The overall mortality rate in that study was 15%, in this one it is 16%. The finding, by Pearson et al. (1992), of significant differences between groups is not replicated. The control group mortality is lower (13%) than the treatment group (18%) although this difference is not significant (TABLE 19).

**TABLE 19**
Mortality

| OUTCOME | TREATMENT N (%) | CONTROL N (%) | ALL N (%) |
|---|---|---|---|
| **Survived** | 58 (82) | 42 (87) | 100 (84) |
| **Died** | 13 (18) | 6 (13) | 19 (16) |
| **Total** | 71 (100) | 48 (100) | 119 (100) |

Fischer's exact test, Sc = 138.5, z = 0.59, $p > 0.05$.

As discussed above, a higher proportion of patients in the treatment group were assessed as suitable pending stability or investigations. It may be that some of the 'excess' mortality can be accounted for in this way. Of the deaths occurring among the treatment group, two occurred before transfer to the unit.

## Complications

Data are available from 100 patients. Approximately half of the missing data (8 cases: 3 control, 6 treatment) was missing because patients had died. The rest of the missing data, from 10 cases, were because notes were not available on the ward at the post-assessment visit and could not be traced later. The most crucial group is, of course, those who died, as it might reasonably be expected that such patients have a higher rate of complications. The proportions lost from each group are approximately equal. However, all analyses where statistical significance is reached have been performed twice, once on the available data and once with the missing data included as 'cases' for each complication. Where this correction (NC) has altered the statistical conclusion it is noted.

The incidence of cases of chest infection is significantly higher in the control group (41%) than the treatment group (15%); see Table 20.

**TABLE 20**

Chest infection

| STATUS | TREATMENT N (N C) (%) | CONTROL N (N C) (%) | ALL N (%) |
|---|---|---|---|
| **Not case** | 53 (85) | 23 (59) | 76 (75) |
| **Case** | 9 (14) (15 ) | 16 (19) (41) | 25 (25) |
| **Total** | 62 (67) (100) | 39 (42) (100) | 101 (100) |

Fischer's exact test Sc = 590.5, z = 2.75, p< 0.01. Data from one patient whose notes were unavailable but whose cause of death was known to be a chest infection are included here. Adjustments are amended accordingly.

Incidence of urinary tract infection also differs significantly between the groups (TABLE 21) with an incidence of 20% in the treatment group and 41% in the control group. This difference is statistically significant before the adjustment for missing data (Fischer's exact test Sc = 458, z = 2.08, $p < 0.05$) but falls just below significance when adjusted (Fischer's exact test Sc = 462.5, z = 1.76, $p > 0.05$).

**TABLE 21**
UTI

| STATUS | TREATMENT N (N C) (%) | CONTROL N (N C) (%) | ALL N (%) |
|---|---|---|---|
| **Not case** | 49 (80) | 23 (59) | 76 (72) |
| **Case** | 12 (18) (20) | 16 (19) (20) | 25 (28) |
| **Total** | 61 (67) (100) | 39 (42) (100) | 100 (100) |

The incidence of diagnosed deep vein thrombosis and pulmonary embolus was low in both groups: treatment group, 3% deep vein thrombosis and 2% pulmonary embolus; control group, 8% deep vein thrombosis and 5% pulmonary embolus (TABLES 22, 23). These differences are not statistically significant.

**TABLE 22**
Deep vein thrombosis

Fischer's exact test Sc = 55, z = 0.55, $p > 0.05$.

| STATUS | TREATMENT N (N C) (%) | CONTROL N (N C) (%) | ALL N (%) |
|---|---|---|---|
| **Not case** | 59 (97) | 36 (92) | 95 (95) |
| **Case** | 2 (8) (3) | 3 (6) (8) | 5 (5) |
| **Total** | 61 (67) (100) | 39 (42) (100) | 100 (100) |

**TABLE 23**
Pulmonary embolus

| STATUS | TREATMENT N (N C) (%) | CONTROL N (N C) (%) | ALL N (%) |
|---|---|---|---|
| **Not case** | 60 (98) | 37 (95) | 97 (97) |
| **Case** | 1 (7) (2) | 2 (5) (5) | 3 (3) |
| **Total** | 61 (67) (100) | 39 (42) (100) | 100 (100) |

Fischer's exact test
Sc = 33, z = 0.39,
p > 0.05.

The incidence of pressure sores differs significantly between groups, with 5% of the treatment group acquiring a pressure sore during the study period compared with 28% of the control group (TABLE 24). The incidence rate in the experimental group as a whole might be regarded as high, although the nature of the patient population in this study is such that many are at high risk of pressure sores for exactly the same reasons that they are deemed suitable for inclusion in the study.

**TABLE 24**
Incidence of pressure sores

| STATUS | TREATMENT N (N C) (%) | CONTROL N (N C) (%) | ALL N (%) |
|---|---|---|---|
| **Not case** | 58 (95) | 28 (72) | 86 (86) |
| **Case** | 3 (9) (5) | 11 (14) (5) | 14 (3) |
| **Total** | 61 (67) (100) | 39 (42) (100) | 100 (100) |

Fischer's exact test
Sc = 504, z = 2.96,
p < 0.01.

Some of the differences noted in these complication rates may account for the differences in abnormal assessment findings (TABLE 25). The difference between the numbers of abnormalities is highly significant (FIGURE 3) with the control group demonstrating far higher levels of abnormal assessment findings.

**TABLE 25**

Number of abnormal assessment findings at discharge

| GROUP | N | MEAN | MEDIAN | TRIMMED MEAN | MINIMUM | MAXIMUM | STANDARD DEVIATION |
|---|---|---|---|---|---|---|---|
| **Treatment** | 57 | 2 | 2 | 2 | 0 | 13 | 2 |
| **Control** | 39 | 7 | 7 | 6 | 0 | 23 | 5 |

**FIGURE 3**

Annotated minitab output from general linear model analysis: abnormalities

| Source | DF | Seq SS | Adj SS | Adj MS | F | P |
|---|---|---|---|---|---|---|
| Group | 1 | 23076 | 3588 | 3588 | 9.86 | 0.002 |
| Pre-test | 1 | 15959 | 14371 | 14371 | 39.47 | 0.000 |
| Group x pre-test | 1 | 107 | 107 | 107 | 0.29 | 0.590 |
| Error | 92 | 33497 | 33497 | 364 | | |
| Total | 95 | 72639 | | | | |

Analysis of covariance for assessment abnormalities post-test. Tests were performed on ranked data.

Test of model abnormalities = group + abnormalities(pre) + group x abnormalities(pre)

The ANCOVA on the raw data gives mean numbers of abnormalities of 2.9 for the treatment group compared with 6.3 for the control group, after adjusting for pre-test differences. The properties of this scale need further exploration.

### Health status and psychological well-being

Unfortunately, it proved impossible to obtain a high response rate to the two questionnaires. Only 45% of patients were able or willing to complete the NHPD (general health status/distress) at pre-test with a slightly lower proportion (42%) completing the GHQ (psychological well-being/distress). This difference is due to the fact that the GHQ was generally presented second. A higher proportion completed the post-test prior to discharge. All available patients were approached (regardless of completion of pre-test) resulting in a total response of 50% (NHPD) and 49% (GHQ). However, the proportion of respondents was much higher in the treatment group. In the treatment group, 39 out of 58 (67%) responded to the NHPD compared with 11 out of 42 (26%) in the control group. Patients on Byron were considerably more accessible to the research team (if only because they were all in one place) and therefore easier to reapproach if assessment was attempted at an inconvenient time for the patient. This does not fully account for the difference. In addition, Byron patients were likely to be more familiar with the researchers because of their relatively frequent presence on the ward. Some of the differences may be accounted for in terms of the different abilities of the groups to complete the questionnaires at post-test related to different outcomes on other variables.

As discussed above, there are no significant differences between the groups in terms of GHQ or NHPD at pre-test There are, however, significant differences at post-test (see TABLE 26). The mean GHQ for the treatment group is lower than the control (i.e. less distress) with a mean score of 2.1, compared with the control of 4.8. As a score of 2 is used as the cut-off point to diagnose potential psychiatric cases in a general population (Goldberg & Williams, 1988), this difference must be regarded as clinically significant, if rather difficult to interpret with such a large proportion of missing data. There is no significant difference in the NHPD between groups (TABLE 26) .

**TABLE 26**

All post-test scores for NHPD and GHQ

| SCALE | GROUP | N | N MISSING | MEAN | MEDIAN | TRIMMED MEAN | STANDARD DEVIATION | MINIMUM | MAXIMUM |
|---|---|---|---|---|---|---|---|---|---|
| **NHPD** | Treatment | 39 | 19 | 6.7 | 6 | 6.4 | 5.8 | 0 | 19 |
| | Control | 11 | 31 | 8.7 | 9 | 8.2 | 6.8 | 0 | 22 |
| **GHQ** | Treatment | 38 | 20 | 2.1 | 1 | 1.8 | 2.9 | 0 | 11 |
| | Control | 11 | 31 | 4.8 | 3 | 4.7 | 3.3 | 1 | 10 |

High score on both scales indicates distress. Range for NHPD 0–24, GHQ 1–12. NHPD: Mann-Whitney $U = 186$, $z_c = -0.782$, $p > 0.05$; GHQ: Mann-Whitney $U = 100$, $z_c = -2.74$, $p < 0.01$.

Only seven members of the control group gave both pre-test and post-test scores (out of a theoretical maximum of 42, i.e. only 16%) whereas 30 members of the control group provided both scores (30 out of 58, i.e. 52%). It was nonetheless felt useful to conduct the planned ANCOVAs.

The analysis of covariance for the NHPD with pre-test score as covariate found no main effect for group, i.e. no evidence of treatment effect (FIGURE 4). The estimated means produced by the raw score version of this model, adjusted for pre-test differences, are almost identical (T = 6.9, C = 7.1).

**FIGURE 4**
ANCOVA on NHPD

Analysis of covariance for NHPD post-test.

Test of model NHPD = group + NHPD(pre) + group x NHPD(pre).

| Source | DF | Seq SS | Adj SS | Adj MS | F | p |
|---|---|---|---|---|---|---|
| Group | 1 | 50.92 | 53.04 | 53.04 | 0.69 | 0.412 |
| Pre-test | 1 | 1513.32 | 443.91 | 443.91 | 5.77 | 0.022 |
| Group x pre-test | 1 | 70.36 | 70.36 | 70.36 | 0.91 | 0.346 |
| Error | 33 | 2538.40 | 2538.40 | 76.92 | | |
| Total | 36 | 4173.00 | | | | |

There was a significant group effect for GHQ (FIGURE 5). Interestingly, the pre-test score is not a significant predictor of the post-test. The main determinant of the score at discharge is thus allocation to experimental group.

**FIGURE 5**
ANCOVA on GHQ

Analysis of covariance for GHQ post test.

Test of model GHQ= group + GHQ(pre) + group x GHQ(pre).

| Source | DF | Seq SS | Adj SS | Adj MS | F | p |
|---|---|---|---|---|---|---|
| Group | 1 | 556.14 | 472.73 | 472.73 | 6.13 | 0.019 |
| Pre-test | 1 | 563.24 | 186.40 | 186.40 | 2.42 | 0.130 |
| Group x pre-test | 1 | 85.94 | 85.94 | 85.94 | 1.12 | 0.299 |
| Error | 32 | 2466.18 | 2466.18 | 77.07 | | |
| Total | 35 | 3671.50 | | | | |

The adjusted means estimated from the raw score version of this model show a large difference, with the treatment group scoring an adjusted mean of 2 compared with the control group's 4.8.

Although the significance of these scores must remain in doubt due to the high attrition and small numbers, the fact that the two scales behave so differently suggests that the results are not simply an artefact of response bias. The higher response from patients on Byron might be an attempt to please the researchers which might in turn bias the scores. This would not tend to affect the two scales differently. However, the results from the scales (which are intended to measure different concepts) do in fact differ. In particular, the concept of psychological well-being might be expected to be more sensitive to nursing care than that of general health status.

## Physical dependence

There is a large difference between groups in levels of physical dependence at discharge (TABLE 27). The mean difference between the groups of 27 points represents a large clinical difference. This difference is also likely to account to some extent for the large difference between groups in proportions of patients going home compared with residential or nursing homes.

TABLE 27

Barthel index scores at discharge

| GROUP | N | MEAN[a] | MEDIAN | TRIMMED MEAN | MINIMUM | MAXIMUM | STANDARD DEVIATION |
|---|---|---|---|---|---|---|---|
| **Treatment** | 58 | 75 | 85 | 78 | 5 | 100 | 23 |
| **Control** | 40 | 48 | 57.5 | 48 | 5 | 100 | 30 |

a Range of Barthel scores is 0–100 where 0 is maximum dependence, 100 is independence.

Analysis of covariance on the ranked data does not reveal the difference to be statistically significant (FIGURE 6). The mean difference for groups adjusted for pre-test difference is 20 points with an adjusted mean for the treatment group of 73 compared with 53 for the control group (FIGURE 6).

FIGURE 6

Annotated minitab output from general linear model analysis

| Source | DF | Seq SS | Adj SS | Adj MS | F | p |
|---|---|---|---|---|---|---|
| Group | 1 | 16501 | 1303 | 1303 | 3.22 | 0.076 |
| Pre-test | 1 | 23366 | 22616 | 22616 | 55.96 | 0.000 |
| Group x pre-test | 1 | 106 | 106 | 106 | 0.26 | 0.609 |
| Error | 94 | 37991 | 37991 | 404 | | |
| Total | 97 | 77964 | | | | |

Analysis of covariance for Barthel post-test.

Test of model Barthel = group + Barthel(pre) + group x Barthel(pre).

The main effect for the experimental group is approaching statistical significance. Applying the ANCOVA to the raw scores does yield a highly statistically significant result, suggesting that the experimental treatment may in fact increase independence. Excluding members of the treatment group who remained in acute wards, the adjusted means remain almost unchanged, with the mean for Byron being 73 compared with 52 for the control group.

A cautious interpretation of these results would suggest that weight should be given to analyses of the ranked score over and above those of the raw score. However, numerous studies have been published utilising raw score data from the Barthel index without much qualm. McDowell & Newell (1987) do, however, make the point that intervals on the scale do not necessarily reflect equal changes in disability. It is probably unsafe to assume that it has the properties of an interval scale, although the reality is that the properties clearly lie between the ordinal and the interval.

## Other therapy

There is no significant difference between the groups in the amount of input from other therapies, with both groups receiving a high level of input (TABLE 28). The level of input is slightly higher than that received prior to the commencement of the study period.

**TABLE 28**

Therapy input during study

| GROUP | N | MEAN | MEDIAN | TRIMMED MEAN | MINIMUM | MAXIMUM | STANDARD DEVIATION |
|---|---|---|---|---|---|---|---|
| **Treatment** | 71 | 3.1 | 3.000 | 3.1 | 0.000 | 6.000 | 1.2 |
| **Control** | 47 | 3.4 | 4.000 | 3.5 | 1.000 | 5.000 | 1.2 |

Mann-Whitney $U = 1338$, $z_c = -1.88$, $p > 0.05$.

Not surprisingly, patients in the control group receive considerably more attention from the medical profession than those in the treatment group (TABLE 29). The control group has nearly five times as many entries made by doctors in the medical record than the treatment group. Most of the difference is accounted for by reviews relating to the admission diagnosis and hence reflects the change in roles and responsibilities, with nursing staff monitoring and reviewing progress along the expected recovery path once medically stable.

**TABLE 29**

Medical reviews

| | | NUMBER OF ENTRIES IN NOTES BY DOCTOR[a] | | NUMBER OF MAJOR REVIEWS[b] | | NUMBER OF REVIEWS RELATING TO ADMISSION DIAGNOSIS[c] | |
|---|---|---|---|---|---|---|---|
| GROUP | N | MEAN | MEDIAN | MEAN | MEDIAN | MEAN | MEDIAN |
| **Treatment** | 57 | 8 | 5 | 1 | 0 | 4 | 2 |
| **Control** | 37 | 28 | 25 | 3 | 2 | 17 | 12 |

a Mann-Whitney $U = 313$, $z_c = -5.7$, $p < 0.01$.

b Mann-Whitney $U = 547$, $z_c = -4.2$, $p < 0.01$.

c Mann-Whitney $U = 486$, $z_c = -4.4$, $p < 0.01$.

There is also a large and statistically significant difference in the number of patients receiving 'major' medical reviews, with a treatment group mean of one compared with three in the control group. This difference is more difficult to account for in terms of expectation as most major reviews relate to unanticipated occurrences such as serious illness or failure to make expected recovery. The figures for the treatment group include the entire hospital stay after referral and hence reflect periods under medically-managed care.

Of the patients transferred to Byron, 16% (10) were referred back for a period under medically-managed care. Of these, half were transferred to another ward and half were managed on Byron.

# References


AUDIT COMMISSION (1992)
*Lying in Wait: the Use of Medical Beds in Acute Hospitals,*
HMSO, London.

BARDER, L., SLIMMER, L. & LASAGE, J. (1994)
*Depression and issues of control among elderly people in health care settings,*
Journal of Advanced Nursing, 20, 597–604.

BERGMAN, R. (1981)
*Accountability – definition and dimensions,*
International Nursing Review, 28(2), 53–59.

BLACK, F. (ED.) (1992)
*Primary Nursing: an Introductory Guide,*
King's Fund Centre, London.

BOND, S., & THOMAS, L. H. (1992)
*Measuring patients' satisfaction with nursing care,*
Journal of Advanced Nursing, 17, 52–63.

BOWMAN, G. S., WEBSTER, R. A. & THOMPSON, D. R. (1991)
*The development of a classification system for nurses' work methods,*
International Journal of Nursing Studies, 28(2), 175–187.

BOWMAN, G. S., MEDDIS, R. & THOMPSON, D. R. (1993)
*An item analysis of a classification system for nurses' work methods,*
Journal of Clinical Nursing, 2, 75–79.

BOWSHER, J., BRAMLETT, M., BURNSIDE, I. M. & GUELDNER, S. H. (1993)
*Methodological considerations in the study of frail elderly people,*
Journal of Advanced Nursing, 18, 873–879.

BRADSHAW, A. (1995)
*Report on the Nurse-Led Beds Unit (unpublished),*
Huddersfield Royal Infirmary NHS Trust, Huddersfield.

COOK, D. C. & CAMPBELL, D. T. (1979)
*Quasi-experimentation: Design and Analysis Issues for Field Settings,*
Houghton Mifflin Co., Boston.

DAVIES, S. M. (1994)
*An evaluation of nurse-led team care within a rehabilitation ward for elderly people,*
Journal of Clinical Nursing, 3, 25–33.

DEPARTMENT OF HEALTH (1993)
*Making London Better,*
Department of Health, Health Publications Unit, Heywood.

DEPARTMENT OF HEALTH (1993)
*Research and Development Priorities in Relation to the Interface between Primary and Secondary Care: Report to the NHS Central R&D Committeee,*
Department of Health, London.

ERSSER, S. (1988)
*Nursing beds and nursing therapy.* In *Primary Nursing: Nursing in the Burford and Oxford Nursing Development Units (A. Pearson, Ed.),* Croom Helm, London.

EVANS, A. (1993)
*Accountability: a core concept for primary nursing,*
Journal of Clinical Nursing, 2, 231–234.

EVANS, A. & GRIFFITHS, P. (1994)
*The Development of a Nursing-Led In-Patient Service,*
King's Fund, London.

EVERITT, B., & DUNN, G. (1983)
*Advanced Methods of Data Exploration and Modelling,*
Heinemann, London.

FITZPATRICK, R. (1990)
*Measurement of patient satisfaction.* In *Measuring the Outcomes of Medical Care (A. Hopkins & D. Costain, Eds),*
Royal College of Physicians of London, Kings Fund, London, pp. 19–26.

GOLDBERG, D. & WILLIAMS, P. (1988)
*A User's Guide to the General Health Questionnaire,*
NFER – Nelson, Windsor.

GRANGER, C., ALBRECHT, G. & HAMILTON, B. (1979A)
*Outcome of comprehensive medical rehabilitation: measurement by PULSES profile and the Barthel index,*
Archives of Physical Medicine and Rehabilitation, 60, 145–154.

GRANGER, C. V., DEWIS, L. S., PETERS, N. C., SHERWOOD, C. C. & BARRETT, J. E. (1979B)
*Stroke rehabilitation: analysis of repeated Barthel index measures,*
Archives of Physical Medicine and Rehabilitation, 60, 14–17.

HALL, L. E. (1969)
*The Loeb Centre for Nursing and Rehabilitation, Montefiore Hospital and Medical Center, Bronx, New York,*
International Journal of Nursing Studies, 6, 81–97.

HALL, L., ALFONS, G., RIFKIN, E. & LEVINE, H. (1975)
*Final Report: Longtitudinal Effects of an Experimental Nursing Process,*
Loeb Centre for Nursing, New York.

HAYWARD, J. (1975)
*Information: a Prescription against Pain,*
Royal College of Nursing, London.

KING'S FUND CENTRE (1989)
*Nursing Development Units – an Idea whose Time has Come,*
unpublished (quoted in Turner Shaw & Bosanquet, 1993).

KING'S FUND INSTITUTE (1994)
*London: the Key Facts – a Briefing Paper about Health and Health Care in London,*
King's Fund Institute, London.

KITSON, A. L. (1986)
*Indicators of quality in nursing care – an alternative approach,*
Journal of Advanced Nursing, 11, 133–144.

KITSON, A. L. (1991)
*Therapeutic Nursing and the Hospitalised Elderly,*
Scutari Press, Harrow.

LEACH, C. (1979)
*Introduction to Statistics: a Non-parametric Approach for the Social Sciences,*
John Wiley & Sons, Chichester.

MACGUIRE, J. (1989A)
*An approach to evaluating the introduction of primary nursing in an acute medical unit for the elderly. II Operationalising the principles,*
International Journal of Nursing Studies, 26(3), 253–260.

MACGUIRE, J. (1989B)
*An approach to evaluating the introduction of primary nursing in an acute medical unit for the elderly. I Principles and practice,*
International Journal of Nursing Studies, 26(3), 243–251.

MAGUIRE, P. A., TAYLOR, I. C. & STOUT, R. W. (1986)
*Elderly patients in acute medical wards: factors predicitng length of stay in hospital,*
British Medical Journal, 292 (10 May), 1251–1253.

MAHONEY, F. I. & BARTHEL, D. W. (1965)
*Functional evaluation: the Barthel index,*
Maryland State Medical Journal, 14, 61–65.

MARKS, L. (1994)
*Seamless Care or Patchwork Quilt? (Research Report No. 17),*
King's Fund, London.

MCDOWELL, I. & NEWELL, C. (1987)
*Measuring Health: a Guide to Rating Scales and Questionnaires,*
Oxford University Press, New York.

MCKENNA, S. P., HUNT, S. M. & TENNANT, A (1993)
*The development of a patient-completed index of distress from the Nottingham Health Profile: a new measure for use in cost-utility studies,*
British Journal of Medical Economics, 6, 13–24.

MCMAHON, R. (1991)
*Therapeutic nursing: theory, issues and practice.* In *Nursing as Therapy (R. McMahon & A. Pearson, Eds),*
Chapman & Hall, London.

McSweeney, P. (1991)
*Patient's distress: an investigation,*
Senior Nurse, 11(4), 17–20, 38.

Mead, D. (1991)
*An evaluation tool for primary nursing,*
Nursing Standard, 6(1), 37–39.

Miller, A. (1985)
*Nurse/patient dependency – is it iatrogenic?*
Journal of Advanced Nursing, 10, 63–69.

Minitab Inc. (1991)
*Minitab Statistical Software,*
State College, PA, USA.

Narain, P., Rubenstein, L. Z., Wieland, D., Rosbrook, B., Strome, S., Pietruszka, F. & Morley, J. E. (1988)
*Predictors of immediate and 6-month outcomes in hospitalized elderly patients: the importance of functional status,*
Journal of the American Geriatrics Society, 36, 775–783.

Naylor, M. D., Munro, B. H. & Brooten, D. A. (1991)
*Measuring the effectiveness of nursing practice,*
Clinical Nurse Specialist, 5(4), 210–215.

Orem, D. (1990)
*Nursing: Concepts of Practice, 4th edition,*
McGraw-Hill, New York.

Pearson, A. (1983)
*The Clinical Nursing Unit,*
William Heinemann Medical Books, London.

Pearson, A. (Ed.) (1987)
*Nursing Quality Measurement: Quality Assurance Methods for Peer Review,*
John Wiley & Sons, Chichester.

Pearson, A. (1989)
*Therapeutic nursing – transforming models and theories in action,*
Recent Advances in Nursing, 24, 123–151.

Pearson, A. (1992)
*Nursing at Burford: a Story of Change,*
Scutari Press, London.

Pearson, A., Punton, S. & Durant, I. (1992)
*Nursing Beds: an Evaluation of the Effects of Therapeutic Nursing,*
Scutari Press, London.

Roper, N., Logan, W. & Tierny, A. (1980)
*The Elements of Nursing,*
Churchill Livingstone, Edinburgh.

Russel, J., Pettersson, G. & Davies, J. (1994)
*Londoners' Views on the Future of Health Care (King's Fund London Initiative Working Paper No.14),*
King's Fund Institute, London.

SEMKE, J., VANDER WEELE, T. & WEATHERLEY, R. (1989)
*Delayed discharges for medical and surgical patients in an acute care hospital,*
Social Work in Health Care, 14(1), 15–31.

STEWART, B. J. & ARCHBOLD, P. G. (1992)
*Focus on psychometrics: nursing intervention studies require outcome measures that are sensitive to change: part 1,*
Research in Nursing and Health, 15, 477–481.

STEWART, B. J. & ARCHBOLD, P. G. (1993)
*Focus on psychometrics: nursing intervention studies require outcome measures that are sensitive to change: part 2,*
Research in Nursing and Health, 16, 77–81.

THOMAS, L. H. & BOND, S. (1990)
*Towards defining the organisation of nursing care in hospital wards: an empirical study,*
Journal of Advanced Nursing, 15, 1106–1112.

TIFFANY, C. (1977)
*Nursing Organisational Structure and the Real Goals of Hospitals: a Correlational Study,* (quoted in Pearson 1989), PhD,
Indiana University.

TURNER SHAW, J. & BOSANQUET, N. (1993)
*A Way to Develop Nurses and Nursing,*
King's Fund Centre, London.

TUTTON, E. (1991)
*An exploration of touch and its use in nursing.* In *Nursing as Therapy (R. McMahon & A. Pearson, Eds),*
Chapman & Hall, London.

VICTOR, C., NAZARETH, B., HUDSON, M. & FULOP, N. (1994)
*The inappropriate use of acute hospital beds in an Inner London District Health Authority.*
Health Trends, 25(3), 94–97.